PLANTING THE DRY SHADE GARDEN

PLANTING THE DRY SHADE GARDEN

The best plants for the toughest spot in your garden

GRAHAM RICE

photography by
judywhite and Graham Rice

TIMBER PRESS
Portland, Oregon

The photographers thank the dry shade plantings
at Willowwood Arboretum in Morris County, Chester, New Jersey,
which reinforce our faith in county parks.

FRONTISPIECE Three dependable dry shade perennials—*Dryopteris,
Heuchera*, and *Pulmonaria*—make an effective combination even
in a narrow bed that is shaded on two sides.

OPPOSITE Even a low stone wall can create enough extra depth of soil to
encourage hostas, pulmonarias, ferns, and other shade-loving plants to
grow more luxuriantly.

PAGE 6 Feathery ferns and glossy hostas surround a stone sculpture; pieces
of garden art such as this can be a valuable enhancement for creating
attractive shade pictures.

PAGE 8 The range of perennials suitable for dry and shady places offer a
thoughtful choice of leaf shapes and colors, and some also feature bright,
graceful flowers.

Photography ©
  judywhite and Graham Rice
  GardenPhotos.com

Published in 2011 by Timber Press, Inc.
The Haseltine Building
133 S.W. Second Avenue, Suite 450
Portland, Oregon 97204-3527
timberpress.com

Printed in China
Fourth printing 2015

Library of Congress Cataloging-in-Publication Data

Rice, Graham.
    Planting the dry shade garden: The best plants for the toughest spot in your garden/Graham
Rice; photography by judywhite and Graham Rice.—1st ed.
        p. cm.
    Includes bibliographical references and index.
    ISBN 978-1-60469-187-0
    1. Gardening in the shade. 2. Shade-tolerant plants. I. Title.
    SB434.7.R53 2011
    635.9′543—dc22   2010053849

A catalog record for this book is also available from the British Library.

For Monty Stokes
Our new generation gardener,
propagated with love by Lizzie
and Carl

CONTENTS

INTRODUCTION

I F YOU'VE EVER HAD the disconcerting experience of see-ing a man peering over your fence, trying to discern what was growing under your big blue Atlantic cedar or your overgrown rhododendrons—I apologize. That was me. And, I have to say, I often realized that nothing at all was growing there. And so this book is for you.

And to those open and generous garden owners who refrain from running outdoors and shouting at nosy gar-den writers trying to see what they're up to behind their fences and hedges, but rather open their gardens to prying poseurs and genuine and admiring seekers of inspiration— I thank you.

Gardeners learn from from the inspired and bizarre things that other gardeners do. And whether it's Pennsylvania's Milford Secret Gardens Tour or Northamptonshire's Oun-dle Open Gardens, America's Gardens Conservancy or the National Gardens Scheme in England and Wales, I've had a chance to see what gardeners on both sides of the Atlantic have done with the dry shade. This has been an invaluable tonic—and in this book I'd like to share what I've learned.

DRY SHADE IS the most inhospitable part of any garden. Faced with what seems to be a lost cause, some gardeners simply admit defeat and use the area for the woodpile or the tool shed. But there is no reason why dry and shady areas cannot be as attractive as the landscaping in other areas of your property.

In fact, it is wasteful and unnecessary to simply abandon dry shady areas as dark deserts—especially in urban gardens where every square foot of planting space is vital. This book reveals the wealth of beautiful and resilient plants that will flourish in this difficult situation. To get started, you'll be able to make the best plant choices if you first understand the growing conditions. Then you can select from the unexpected and wonderful variety of suitable plants so that the dry and shady parts of the garden can be as lovely as everywhere else.

To grow well, plants need both light and moisture, so the implication is that in dry shady situations they have neither and will not grow. Not so, and I'll explain why in the following pages.

ALL SHADE IS NOT EQUAL

Shade can be cast by solid barriers like walls and fences, by trees, and by overhanging roofs and other structures. It can be solid or dappled, and even some areas that are almost permanently shaded from the direct sun can still be quite bright. Understanding what type of shade you have is the first step in knowing what to plant there.

Fences, Walls, and Buildings

Gardens shaded by solid structures like walls and buildings experience very different conditions from those in shade cast by trees or large shrubs. First, the areas alongside west- and east-facing walls or fences remain shadowed for part of the day but are in good light for the rest of the day. A vast variety of plants will thrive there. North-facing fences and walls, however, are different.

In winter, north-facing borders are sunless. Not only that, but in cold-winter areas, the lack of late winter and spring sun means that this is the last place in the garden where the snow melts and the soil thaws. Late frosts persist for days when in other parts of the garden buds are bursting. There's a benefit however: the quick morning thaw of frosted buds and shoots that is so damaging to camellias and new spring growth never happens; they thaw slowly and open late but remain undamaged.

In summer, things change. In northern latitudes, even in the height of summer, the sun may hang so low in the sky that parts of the planting area close to the wall remain entirely sunless. Farther south, with the sun high, plants shaded in winter may well be subjected to the full force of the sun in high summer.

But, even when shaded, plantings alongside a wall or fence grow in far better light than those under cover of trees. They may have little light, but they are not in the dark, and they often are spared the intense sunlight they cannot tolerate.

Hostas with no variegation, or that are only modestly variegated, fare better in dry shade situations than those dominated by bold white or yellow coloring.

And there is no competition from nearby tree roots for moisture and nutrients.

However, planting areas shaded by walls and fences can be dry. Depending on the prevailing winds, the plants may be struggling in a rain shadow, an area of soil from which rain is largely deflected by a barrier such as a wall or overhang. In planting areas backed by stone or brick walls, the drought is exacerbated when the heat retained in the wall increases evaporation from the soil alongside. This has an impact on vines, wall shrubs, and other plants whose roots compete for the moisture in the soil.

Shade plants like ferns and hostas often thrive in planting areas shaded by buildings, walls, or fences because although they are shaded for much of the day they are open to overhead light.

Under Trees

The degree of moisture available to plants growing under trees is not immediately apparent; there are many variables. And shade from evergreen trees is very different to shade from deciduous trees.

EVERGREEN TREES Broadleaf and coniferous evergreens retain their leaves in all seasons and so they cast shade year-round. This shade may be thinner in winter, depending on when a particular evergreen tree drops its leaves (as do all evergreens at some point during the year), but there is no bright respite for the plants below. The ground flora in coniferous forests can be almost non-existent, not only because so little light reaches the forest floor but because the roots of so many trees in close proximity extract so much of the moisture that reaches the ground.

Most gardeners, however, do not have to contend with a coniferous forest in their backyard. A specimen evergreen tree or a tall rhododendron is more typical and less of a challenge than a true woodland. What the gardener is faced with, in effect, is a circular stretch of forest edge and in a natural setting, the edge of the forest is often an especially floriferous part of the landscape.

Evergreen trees vary in the degree of shade they cast and the amount of moisture they extract from the upper levels of the soil. This partly depends on the sheer denseness of the leaf cover and also on the natural habit of the tree. Trees like the evergreen, or Holm, oak (*Quercus ilex*), the larger evergreen hollies (*Ilex aquifolium, I. ×altaclerensis*), Southern magnolia (*Magnolia grandiflora*), mountain laurel (*Kalmia latifolia*), and some tall rhododendrons cast very dense shade

Ground cloaking *Epimedium ×perralchicum* 'Fröhnleiten' efficiently smothers weeds around a specimen hosta and phormium in a shady yard.

and only by removing low branches can you let in enough light for plants to grow.

Not all evergreens are problematic. Gardeners on the west coast of North America and milder parts of the British Isles can usually grow eucalyptus. These are generally upright in growth and often have thin crowns, so even when they develop a spreading crown they cast only light shade. However, in drier areas of California it is unwise to plant eucalpytus as not only are some species invasive, but they are also highly flammable.

Deciduous trees The shade cast by deciduous trees varies according to species. In general, trees that are climax species—those that dominate in the mature forest—have the most dense canopy of foliage and allow the least light to penetrate below. They become the dominant species partly because they outcompete earlier species in the succession, such as birches. Choosing plants to thrive under these trees needs careful thought,

The drawback of otherwise desirable broadleaf evergreens like mountain laurel (*Kalmia latifolia*) is the dense shade they cast.

but most of those recommended in this book are suitable.

Dense Shade Trees
Garden plants struggle under deciduous trees that cast dense shade. These trees include both forest climax species and those with especially generous leaf cover.

Acer campestre (hedge maple)
Acer pseudoplatanus (sycamore maple)
Aesculus hippocastanum (horse chestnut)
Aesculus indica (Indian horse chestnut)
Carpinus betulus (hornbeam)
Carya cordiformis (bitternut)
Castanea sativa (sweet chestnut)
Fagus americana (American beech)
Fagus sylvatica (European beech)
Magnolia acuminata (cucumber tree)
Magnolia grandiflora (Southern magnolia)
Malus species and cultivars (crabapple)
Parrotia persica (Persian ironwood)
Platanus ×*hispanica* (London plane)
Prunus cultivars (flowering cherry)
Pyrus communis (common pear)
Quercus rubra (red oak)
Salix ×*sepulcralis* var. *chrysocoma* (weeping willow)
Sorbus domestica (service tree)

Light Shade Trees
Deciduous trees that cast lighter shade tend to mature earlier in the succession of forest development and are then themselves often outshaded by climax species. Choosing plants to grow in the shade of these species is less challenging than under dense shade trees.

Acer griseum (paperbark maple)
Amelanchier species (shadblow, serviceberry)
Betula species (birches)

The relatively light shade cast by paperbark maple (*Acer griseum*) makes it a good companion for shade-tolerant plants like hostas.

Though they cast less shade, most birches, including the paper birch (*Betula papyrifera*), have shallow root systems that draw moisture from the soil and so restrict the supply to other plants.

Light shade trees (*continued*)
Broussonetia papyrifera (paper mulberry)
Celtis species (hackberry)
Cercis siliquastrum (Judas tree)
Cornus florida (flowering dogwood)
Cornus nuttallii (Pacific dogwood)
Fraxinus excelsior (European ash)
Ginkgo biloba (maidenhair tree)
Gleditsia triacanthos (honey locust)
Gymnocladus dioicus (Kentucky coffeetree)
Koelreuteria paniculata (goldenrain tree)
Laburnum anagroides (common laburnum)
Larix decidua (European larch)
Meliosma veitchiorum
Phellodendron amurense (Amur cork tree)
Prunus persica (peach)
Robinia pseudoacacia (black locust)
Sophora japonica (Japanese pagoda tree)
Sorbus aucuparia (mountain ash)
Sorbus vestita (Himalayan whitebeam)

SEASONAL SHADE Evergreen trees, of course, cast shade year-round. Deciduous trees are naked in winter, and many shade-tolerant plants deserve that label only because they leaf out and flower before deciduous trees have developed their spring canopy overhead. So its important to note when spring deciduous trees come into leaf.

DECIDUOUS, EARLY-LEAFING TREES
These are the most challenging deciduous trees under which to plant. Trees that start to develop their canopy early have an advantage in the succession as they restrict the light available to all those plants that send out their leaves later. Some of the same species that develop a dense canopy also leaf out early.

Acer platanoides (Norway maple)
Aesculus flava (yellow buckeye)

Aesculus hippocastanum (horse chestnut)
Betula pendula (silver birch)
Carpinus betulus (European hornbeam)
Crataegus monogyna (common hawthorn)
Fagus sylvatica (European beech)
Laburnum anagroides (common laburnum)
Malus species and cultivars (crabapple)
Populus trichocarpa (black cottonwood)
Salix alba var. *vitellina* (golden willow)
Tilia ×*europaea* (lime)

DECIDUOUS, LATE-LEAFING TREES
Trees that begin to leaf out relatively late in the spring allow understory plants to enrich themselves with light and moisture for longer.

Acer griseum (paperbark maple)
Broussonetia papifyra (paper mulberry)
Carya cordiformis (bitternut)
Catalpa bignonoides (Indian bean tree)
Cladrastis lutea (yellow-wood)
Cladrastis sinensis (Chinese yellow-wood)
Cornus nuttallii (Pacific dogwood)
Diospyros lotus (date palm)
Gymnocladus dioicus (Kentucky coffeetree)
Koelreuteria paniculata (goldenrain tree)
Magnolia acuminata (cucumber tree)
Meliosma veitchiorum
Picrasma quassioides (quassia)
Robinia pseudoacacia (black locust)
Sophora japonica (Japanese pagoda tree)
Sorbus vestita (Himalayan whitebeam)

BEST SHADE TREES
Some of the trees on the preceding lists both have foliage that emerges relatively late—giving plants below good early-season light—and also form relatively thin canopies, so they cast lighter shade even in the height of summer. If you are planting new trees in the shade garden, these are the best choices.

Best shade trees (*continued*)
Acer griseum (paperbark maple)
Broussonetia papifyra (paper mulberry)
Cornus nuttallii (Pacific dogwood)
Gymnocladus dioicus (Kentucky coffeetree)
Koelreuteria paniculata (goldenrain tree)
Meliosma veitchiorum
Robinia pseudoacacia (black locust)
Sophora japonica (Japanese pagoda tree)
Sorbus vestita (Himalayan whitebeam)

WORST SHADE TREES
The foliage of some trees emerges relatively early and restricts early-season light to the plants below; it also forms a relatively dense canopy that casts heavy shade. These are the least appropriate trees to choose when planting trees for a new shade garden and they are the toughest deciduous trees under which to plant.

Acer platanoides (Norway maple)
Aesculus hippocastanum (horse chestnut)
Carpinus betulus (hornbeam)
Fagus sylvatica and cultivars (European beech)
Malus species and cultivars (crabapple)
It is also inadvisable to plant walnuts (*Juglans* species) as their root secretions are toxic to some plants.

CROWN SHAPES
There is also one more basic and perhaps more immediately obvious issue—the shape of a tree's crown. Trees with relatively broad, spreading crowns cast more shade than upright trees. Weeping cultivars also cut out much of the light from the side, creating very dark conditions. For example, a weeping purple beech, *Fagus sylvatica* 'Purpurea Pendula', is impossible to plant beneath; it has a dense, early-closing canopy, branches that weep to the ground, *and* dark foliage that reflects no light.

Trees and Moisture
Trees, of course, also have an impact on soil moisture—in two ways. In shaded conditions less moisture evaporates from the soil surface and less water vapor transpires from the foliage of plants in the shade garden. However, this is more than counterbalanced by the vast amount of moisture tree roots take in, moisture that is therefore not available to perennials and shrubs below. And, here again, there are differences between tree species. It is sometimes suggested that deep-rooted trees are more appropriate for shade gardens than shallow-rooted ones because deep roots provide less competition for understory plants. But, in truth, the situation is more nuanced.

ROOT SYSTEMS
Most trees develop root systems that are concentrated in the upper layers of the soil, where the most humus and nutrients are to be found. Also, a widely spreading, shallow root system is very effective in keeping a large tree stable. Some trees, especially on very light sandy soils, will also develop a vertical tap root for additional stability. But in general it is more a case of the roots of some trees being shallower than the roots of others, rather than the roots of some trees being deeper and those of others being shallow.

DEEPER-ROOTED TREES
Carya species (hickory)
Quercus alba (white oak)
Nyssa sylvatica (black gum)
Sassafras albidum (sassafras)
Sophora japonica (Japanese pagoda tree)

The root systems of dogwoods are shallow and may compete for moisture and nutrients with the plants beneath. But their airy canopies allow hostas, ferns, and columbines to thrive in the semi-shade conditions.

Shallow-rooted Trees

Acer japonicum (Japanese maple)

Acer rubrum (red maple)

Betula species (birches)

Celtis occidentalis (hackberry)

Cornus (dogwood)

Populus deltoides (cottonwood)

Salix species (willows)

Root extension—the myth exposed Another misconception is that the roots of a mature tree extend out from the trunk for about the same distance as the branches, and this allows the fine roots to take in the moisture that drips on to the soil from the outer foliage. In fact, tree roots often extend much farther and not always evenly. Roots will tend to develop more strongly, for example, in patches of fertile soil, and a cursory glance may not always reveal where these are. Roots try to find areas alongside paths and driveways where water runs off; if you create a new planting bed in the sun beyond the canopy, you may well find it occupied by the roots of trees that do not overhang the bed.

Beneath the canopy, especially towards the trunk, dry conditions are as much the result of rain failing to penetrate the canopy as roots extracting moisture from the soil. The same

Although rain running down a tree's trunk can provide needed moisture for the soil at its base, it can also wash away the dirt, leaving the tree's roots exposed.

trees with a sparse canopy that creates dappled shade also allow more rain to penetrate to the soil beneath. Moisture evaporates off the foliage of dense canopies and may also run back down the branches and the trunk, soaking in at the base of the tree and leaving little moisture in the soil.

WATER UPTAKE Trees also take up water at variable rates. In early winter and midwinter, deciduous trees are relatively dormant but start to absorb more moisture as winter slides into spring and the demands of thirsty new spring growth dominate. In the fall, water use declines again.

Evergreens tend to follow a less clear-cut version of the same pattern.

Rapidly growing trees use more moisture than slower-growing trees of a similar size or age, so fast-growing young birches take up far more water than slow-growing young oaks. Eventually, however, the oaks will overtop the birches and dominate the canopy.

Now that you understand the variability of shade and dry conditions, you can improve the site so that an unexpected range of plants can be grown.

WHETHER YOU CHOOSE a blanket of ground cover or the delightful intricacies of a richly planted shade garden to enhance the dry, shady areas of your property, it all starts with broadening the choice of available plants. That depends on making the area less shady and less dry.

REDUCING SHADE

Structural features like tall walls, roof overhangs, or the corners where fences or walls meet are impossible to change. The only solution is to choose plants that will cope with the situation. But shade under trees is different.

Existing mature trees that cast an uncomfortable degree of shade can be dealt with in one of three ways. The tree can be removed entirely. This is a good option for trees past maturity—which, for trees such as Japanese cherries, may be only 25 to 30 years—and for trees that have suffered severe storm damage or ruinous unskilled pruning. Sometimes you have to be ruthless—a tree is supposed to be a restful and elegant garden feature, not an eyesore. However, tree removal may prove to be an expensive option.

The opposite alternative is to do nothing. Some maturing trees are best left to stand in their glory. If the shade they cast is so dense that few plants will tolerate it, then use those few plants in as many forms as you can find. If the shade is all-embracing—as it may be from a weeping beech, or a really dense Japanese maple, for example—then appreciate that this is the price you pay for the good fortune of having a mature specimen to admire.

The middle way is to undertake some thoughtful pruning. By that I do not mean that you should get up on a rickety ladder with a carpentry saw and a bucketful of overconfidence. And neither should you entrust the work to a call-at-the-door-on-the-off-chance "tree surgeon" whose expertise may be on the same level as yours but his confidence even more ruinously excessive. Ominously, there will also be a very large chainsaw in the back of his truck. And several empty beer cans. And no medical kit. And no insurance.

It is perfectly possible to tackle small trees yourself—trees that are, as you might say, more like a shrub on a stick than a tree. And some carefully considered thinning of the crown in the young life of a tree may ensure that it casts less-dense shade as it grows. A good guide is that if you need a full-size ladder rather than a set of steps or a small stepladder: hire an expert. In America, be sure to choose a certified, bonded arborist. In Britain, choose a qualified, certified tree surgeon. And as with any landscaping professional, always check their references.

Reducing the amount of shade cast by a tree can be done in two ways: crown thinning and crown lifting. Crown thinning involves reducing the total number of large branches; crown lifting means removing lower branches.

CROWN THINNING A professional will thin the crown of a mature or maturing tree by

Shade from evergreen trees like this Japanese fir, *Abies firma*, can be overpowering, but by pruning up the lower branches you will allow enough light to grow hostas and epimediums.

thoughtfully removing whole branches. The aim is retain the overall shape of the tree but with fewer branches so the tree casts less shade. It is often easier to make an assessment of the appropriate branches to remove in winter, because you have a clear view of the complete branch structure—on deciduous trees at least. The pruning is usually best done in late winter or, in the case of cherries (*Prunus*), in late spring. The goal is not to leave stumps or bark tears, and when the tree leafs out in spring it should look as good as it did before but allow more light to penetrate below.

If you are pruning a small tree yourself, follow the standard pruning guidelines: removing limbs that are damaged, diseased, dead, or crossing and rubbing. Then consider if there are branches that are badly shaped or have narrow crotches and so be more likely to split in windy conditions. In some cases this may be enough pruning, but never remove more than about a quarter of a tree's growth or the overall health of the plant may be compromised.

CROWN LIFTING The second approach is crown lifting—perhaps more appealingly referred to as "raising the skirt." Crown lifting involves removing branches from low down on the tree to let in more light from the side. Removing the lower branches also reduces the physical damage they can do to smaller plants as they sweep back and forth in summer breezes. Some trees, like cedars and other conifers, rely on their full complement of branches to create their elegant appearance and can be ruined by this treatment. But for oaks, most limes (*Tilia*), large maples, and the like it can work well. Remove only as many branches as needed to solve the problem. Don't reduce the tree to little more than a tuft on a pole.

Removing large branches is a skilled job, even when those branches are low on the tree. The best time to assess your trees is in late summer. The full weight of foliage will bring the branches down so you can evaluate their lowest point. Removing the branches at this time of year usually causes no bleeding of sap, and calluses will start to form before winter.

When planting a new tree, you can plan ahead by removing some of the lower branches at this early stage. As the tree matures, it develops a high crown without the need for major surgery in later years.

INCREASING MOISTURE

Increasing the moisture content of the soil is even more important than decreasing the amount of shade. This can be achieved in one of four ways, or these different approaches can be combined:

- Raise the soil level.
- Improve the soil.
- Install irrigation.
- Mulch regularly.

RAISED BEDS Simply dumping a few yards of additional soil on a problem area is not usually the the best way to raise the soil level. It is far more effective—and attractive—to build a raised bed and fill it with humus-rich, water-retentive soil that creates a better environment for plants.

Depending on your garden style, a raised bed can be as simple as a few logs laid on the ground (oak will last especially well). Or you can build a bed using almost any landscaping material: logs cut into rounds, new or used lumber, stone, bricks, or concrete blocks—or other locally available materials.

The shallow roots of Japanese maples (*Acer palmatum*) not only compete with the roots of perennials and bulbs, but are also easily damaged if you plant underneath the tree. Some gardeners opt to simply enjoy the tree as a specimen.

Removing the lower branches on this fir, *Picea*, will brighten the
planting area below and allow a wider range of plants to be grown.

Logs more than 1 ft. (30 cm) in diameter and 6 ft. (2 m) long are difficult to handle, but even at that size they are one of the simplest and quickest borders for a raised bed. Set them in place, mark where they rest on the ground, roll them out of the way, and dig a trench a couple of inches deep. Then roll the logs back into the trench, which will keep them in place. For additional stability you can also hammer in some wooden or steel stakes behind the logs, where they will be concealed, and secure them to the logs using straps or long brass or stainless steel screws. Logs set upright are more suited to steep slopes but will rot more quickly because the wet soil is directly in contact with the cut surface of the wood.

Rot-resistant rough cut or planed boards, set on edge, are also more formal than logs and can be bent to follow a curved line. If you prefer not to use older pressure-treated lumber, a range of safer non-copper-based options can be found at most lumberyards and building centers. Secure the boards in place with sturdy stakes or metal posts in the inside corners or edges of the bed. In very cold areas frost heave may loosen the stakes if they are not set deeply—but this can be difficult in soil full of tree roots.

Stone can make a good low wall, but building a dry stone wall needs skill to create an attractive and stable structure. Bricks and blocks are easier options for more formal or contemporary landscapes.

Building a low raised bed, such as this one bordered with oak logs and filled with new planting soil, can significantly expand the range of plants that you can grow.

You can build a raised bed as much as 2 ft. (60 cm) high, but 1 ft. (30 cm) is usually sufficient, easier to build, and more stable. Trees may suffer if soil is piled deeply over their roots as it will interfere with oxygen levels in the soil; 9 to 12 in. (22 to 30 cm) is better for the tree. Never mound more than a few inches of soil directly against the trunk of the tree and always leave a gap between the edges of a raised bed and a tree trunk. Keep the space clear of debris.

IMPROVING SOIL Fill raised beds with a moisture-retentive soil mix that drains well. Woodland plants prefer a soil that retains water, but retaining too much moisture can be counterproductive, so the soil must also be well-drained. A mixture of equal parts by volume of topsoil and organic matter works well. The availability of organic matter varies by region, but you can choose from used seed and potting soil, composted pine bark, composted wood waste (often branded and bagged at the garden center), uncolored mulch, well-rotted manure, and leaf mold. Some gardeners add gravel to the mix to ensure good drainage. Others simply use topsoil, with no additional organic matter, especially if they will be planting adaptable shrubs or a robust ground cover rather than a collection of more choice cultivars.

To prevent—or at least delay—the roots of nearby trees from invading the bed, cover the ground with stout but permeable landscape fabric before filling with soil mix. Then blend the ingredients of your soil mix and fill the bed half-way. Tamp down the soil, fill to the top, tamp again, and top off.

If you have a small, sloping, or otherwise tricky area, you may choose simply to spread the soil mix over the area without bothering to create a true raised bed. This is easy and quick, and once robust ground cover plants are established, may be sufficient to transform the area for relatively little time and cost.

Amending the soil itself is also crucial and is a necessary preparation before all planting. In areas where tree roots are troublesome, forking over the soil to add organic matter may be impossible so spreading new soil on the surface or making a raised bed will be the solution. In planting areas shaded not by trees but by structures, there may well be no tree roots so amending the soil will not be difficult.

INSTALLING IRRIGATION The most basic answer to dry soil under trees, in the shade of structures or indeed anywhere in the garden is irrigation. And by that I do not mean sprinklers. The vast majority of the water that comes out of a sprinkler evaporates before it ever reaches the soil, so the aquifers are drained for no good reason. It's not selfish, it's not thoughtless—it's just not wise.

Instead, use some form of automatic irrigation, such as soaker hoses or drip irrigation. Soaker hoses are micro-perforated black pipes, usually made of recycled car tires. Drip irrigation consists of flexible PVC tubing with emitters that deliver water where directed. Neither system is expensive, nor is it difficult to install. You simply lay the hose or tubing directly on the soil where you wish to irrigate, connect it to the water supply, and moisture soaks directly into the soil, with very little wasteful evaporation. Covering the soaker hose or tubing with mulch conceals it and ensures that even more moisture is retained.

Connect your irrigation system to an outside faucet and install a timer to ensure that the water is turned on regularly. It is crucial that irrigation is thorough. Give too little, so that moisture only soaks in a few inches, and the tree roots will creep towards the surface in search of it. The whole area will soon be full of roots. So leave the irrigation on for an hour and a half, and then wait for the soil to start to dry out before soaking it again. Irrigating in this way is the single most important thing you can do to transform inhospitable dry shade into moist shade—the perfect home for so many plants.

MULCHING We have become used to the idea of regular mulching, which is essentially the horticultural replication of natural forest conditions. It increases the humus level of the soil and improves its structure over the long term, helps keep down weeds and prevents the germination of their seeds, and greatly improves the look of the garden. In particular, of course, it also helps to retain moisture in the soil.

So what are the best materials? We can all agree that hideous orange mulch is the scourge of suburbia. Beyond that, there is no perfect mulch for the shade garden, simply a range of compromises from which to choose. Options vary in different regions; choose local materials if possible.

MULCH MATERIALS

- **AGRICULTURAL PLANT WASTES AND BY-PRODUCTS** Check for local availability of corn husks, peanut hulls, nut shells, and similar products. Often a very economical local option; varies in appearance and permanence.

1. To build a more formal planting bed, set treated boards on edge and secure with stakes or posts fastened to the inside of the boards.

2. Fill the new bed with fresh soil; it will conceal the posts. A flat stone at the bed's end provides a naturalistic touch.

- Bark chips Widely available; mostly resistant to decay. Hardwood bark breaks down more quickly than softwood bark. Appearance is good, but can be coarse; cannot usually be produced at home.
- Composted household waste Increasingly seen in or near urban areas; environmentally valuable; breaks down quickly; often an economical local option.
- Composted pine bark My top choice—but expensive and not available in all areas. Has fine texture, good natural color, and breaks down slowly. Can also be used for soil amendment.
- Composted sewage sludge Increasingly seen in or near urban areas; sustainable; breaks down quickly. May be blended with other materials.
- Garden compost Unpredictable quality; breaks down quickly and is full of weed seeds if not made well. Better used to prepare your vegetable beds.
- Grass clippings The worst option. Clippings are not attractive and, if too thick, rot down slowly. The decomposing grass robs the soil of nitrogen and invariably contains many weed seeds. Compost your lawn clippings instead.
- Home-chipped wood waste Chipped

The most water-efficient and consistent way to water plants in a shade garden is through the use of a soaker hose. Conceal the hose with mulch.

Long straight runs of ½-in. (12-mm) drip irrigation line are useful for large planting areas. Many different types of emitters can be fitted into the lines.

prunings and small branches; if foliage is included, has useful nitrogen content. Drawbacks are that chipping machines are noisy and many are gas guzzlers.

- PEAT MOSS Environmentally unsound; breaks down slowly; looks good when moist but can be so fine that it blows away when dry. Best avoided.
- PINE NEEDLES Only available in some areas; look good in appropriate settings, such as near conifers; break down fairly quickly.
- SAWDUST AND OTHER WOOD WASTE Available in some areas; breaks down quickly but robs the soil of nitrogen.

- SHREDDED LEAVES Best home-produced option. Leaves are widely available and it seems fitting that the shade trees that are creating such a problem will also be providing a solution. Good-looking, breaks down quickly. Do not mulch with unshredded leaves. Power leaf shredders are noisy and drink gas.
- WOOD CHIPS Available in some areas; texture variable, can be too coarse, but often looks good. Rots more quickly than bark chips and robs the soil of nitrogen.

So my top options are composted pine bark and shredded leaves. They both look natural and can

Mulch really is a necessity for dry, shady beds. The ideal, however, is to gradually "fill in the blanks" so that you are looking at plants rather than exposed bark mulch.

be forked into the soil as an amendment before you replenish the surface mulch. Both will rot down in time and help enrich the soil. They provide a good visual background for plants and their fine texture allows plants like *Chionodoxa* to penetrate easily as they emerge in spring. Unfortunately, composted pine bark is not always available, and can be expensive; leaves are freely available—but they need shredding.

How to mulch There are many factors that determine how much mulch to apply and when to do so. New gardeners and overenthusiastic landscape contractors tend to over-mulch; more experienced gardeners may tend to under-mulch, feeling that small plants will be smothered and never emerge.

The depth of mulch matters. Where shrubs and stout perennials dominate the planting, the mulch can be 3 in. (7.5 cm) deep; where you have planted dwarf bulbs like snowdrops and small spring perennials including lamiums and epimediums, 2 in. (5 cm) is plenty.

In relatively warm-winter climates, like Britain and the Pacific Northwest, mulches are often applied in late winter when the soil is moist following winter rains. However, with some early plants like hellebores and snowdrops already in growth, timing can depend on the plants around which the mulch is to be spread. In general, apply mulch when plants are dormant.

In areas with cold winters, applying mulch in the fall provides an insulating barrier against frost and tends to moderate the ground temperature through the winter, reducing frost heave. In late fall, after you have tidied away all dying herbaceous material and weeds, apply the mulch as your final task of the season.

SHADY CONTAINERS

Taking a completely different approach, containers can be used to bring color to dry shade. This allows you to grow colorful or interesting plants in good soil and to keep them well watered. There are two approaches: you can maintain containers as season-long features, or feature them in rotation for shorter periods. Depending on individual circumstances, plants can be brought towards maturity in more agreeable conditions, moved into position for a month, then swapped and given better conditions in which to recover before being moved back.

It pays to set each container on a slab. Lightweight plastic containers make for less strenuous moving; use soilless potting mix for the same reason. Containers can also be hidden to allow ornamental plants to grow without root competition from surrounding trees. For example, inset a plastic window box in dense ground cover such as pachysandra.

Container Plants for Shade

In all cases it pays to keep the design simple. Here are a few suggestions.

- Brightly colored, large-leaved forms of *Heuchera* such as 'Citronelle', 'Lime Marmalade', or ×*Heucherella* 'Brass Lantern' or 'Stoplight'.
- Specimen-sized plants of genuine dry shade lovers like the elegant *Carex pendula*, or perhaps its variegated form 'Moonraker'.
- Galvanized steel baths planted with individual cultivars of *Impatiens* in pale colors.
- Trailing hardy geraniums like 'Rozanne' or 'Blue Sunrise' can be good short-term dry shade container plants.

Set pots of shade-loving plants like *Heuchera* directly in the border to fill any seasonal gaps.

Hostas are ideal sculptural container plants. This study in blue combines a
potted hosta with an azure urn in the corner of a sheltered patio.

• Tubs of silvered ivies such as 'Eva' or 'Glacier', their stems trailing over the sides.

In many situations the best approach to turning an inhospitable area of dry shade into an attractive and interesting shade garden is to combine all these solutions: create a raised bed and fill with a high-humus soil mix, set up an automatic watering system, and apply a mulch over the top. Set aside one or two positions for containers. The result will be a shade garden that provides a genuine opportunity to create an attractive planting of colorful and intriguing plants that entices rather than discourages visitors.

CHOOSING PLANTS FOR DRY SHADE

TURNING AN UNAPPEALING dry shade area into an attractive planting is a joint venture between the gardener and the plants. The gardener works hard to improve the conditions, the plants work hard to grow in the conditions that the gardener provides. But choosing the right plants is crucial.

Obviously, plants that demand bright light and constant moisture are foolish choices for dry shade. In fact, most of the plants that thrive in dry and shady situations do so because they are adapted to grow in similar situations in their natural habitats.

To cope with the drought we need to choose from plants that:

• Tend to lose less moisture through their leaves than most plants.
• Have roots, rhizomes, tubers, stems, or other organs that tend to store water.

To cope with low light levels we need to choose from plants that:

• Are evergreen, so can make the most of available light at any time of year.
• Start their annual life cycle early, so collect as much light as possible early in the season when the leaf canopy overhead is still thin.
• Are adapted to growing in low-light conditions.

Fortunately, the plants that meet these conditions are not all boring evergreens that simply produce more and more dull foliage. There are some real sparklers, and this book highlights some of the best.

A note on natives

With the continuing enthusiasm for growing native plants in gardens, it makes sense to look to our native British and American floras to find plants which grow in dry shade in the wild. There are some valuable examples, and these are listed at the end of my choice of plants.

However, although we are aware of the value of natives, we should also be aware that occasional garden plants suited to dry shade may be invasive in some regions and some circumstances. The majority of plants are perfectly safe, and no plants are invasive everywhere. I have noted those plants that have a tendency to overstep their bounds, but check with some reliable local sources for plants that may be problematic in your area.

PREVIOUS The slender divisions in the foliage of *Helleborus foetidus* combine well with the broader leaves of heucheras, which come in so many leaf shades and patterns.

RIGHT The small, even foliage and neat habit of boxwoods such as 'Green Velvet' contrast well with the texture of larger-leaved epimediums and hostas.

Aucuba japonica

Reliable evergreen for foliage and fruits

Bold and resilient evergreen shrubs reaching to 10 ft. (3 m) in height, with some dwarf cultivars. The large, glossy, deep green leaves are up to 8 in. (20 cm) long and vary from broadly oval to long and narrow; they may be splashed with yellow, speckled with gold, or both—some heavily, others more delicately. On female plants, the small, unremarkable spring flowers are followed by clusters of bright red berries, but a nearby male plant is needed to ensure fruiting. Always buy a named cultivar to be sure of getting the male or female you need. Confusingly, both male and female forms may be found under some older names; it takes only one slapdash nursery to assume that because the foliage looks the same, the plants are the same. The self-fertile 'Rozannie' is probably the best choice for smaller sites, but this too fruits more prolifically with the presence of a male plant.

Height 10 ft. (3 m)
Hardiness Z6

WHEN A PLANT is recognized as both attractive and dependable, it becomes widely planted. Such are the whims of gardeners that, after a spell in the spotlight, this very ubiquity sparks disdain. Hence the fate of the spotted laurel.

First introduced into the west from Japan as long ago as 1783, it was indeed a spotted form, *Aucuba japonica* 'Variegata', that was the first to be widely grown. It received an award—a First Class Certificate, no less—from the Royal Horticultural Society in 1865. 'Variegata', 'Grandis', with large plain green leaves, and the more slender-leaved 'Lancifolia', became staple plantings for many decades before the tide turned. Declared "boring" by gardeners, until recently aucubas were being torn out of shrub borders, mixed borders, informal hedges, windbreaks, and soundscreens. But it was no accident that in dry shady places they outlasted their neighbors. Rather than being scorned, they should have been admired and, fortunately, gardeners are once again starting to recognize the value of these shrubs.

All forms are excellent dry shade plants for zone 6 and above. In the darkest and driest sites, those with broad, plain green leaves will be more successful than those with narrow, heavily speckled or variegated foliage. Fortunately, aucubas provide enough variety in foliage form and pattern, and even in fruit color, that larger dry shade gardens can benefit from more than one cultivar.

Use spotted laurel along boundaries as a background to smaller shrubs, perennials, and bulbs; they are also ideal shrubs to soften corners in urban gardens. They make fine large foundation plants for the north side of the house, and even in dry shade are sufficiently dense to buffer noise from roads and neighbors. Display their foliage and fruits in large arrangements; they will outlast any flowers paired with them.

Aucuba japonica 'Pepper Pot' is more densely and evenly speckled with yellow than older spotted types.

Bold, buttery yellow splashes on the foliage of *Aucuba japonica* 'Picturata' result in a plant that is very colorful, but slower growing.

RECOMMENDED SELECTIONS

Just remember that you need a male (♂) to ensure fruits on the female (♀).

Aucuba japonica **'Crotonifolia'** Large leaves with bold gold spots and blotches; one of the most colorful of all aucubas. ♀

Aucuba japonica **'Fructo-albo'** Dark leaves thinly speckled in pale green and gold; cream-colored fruits. ♀

Aucuba japonica **'Gold Dust'** The most brightly speckled female form. Red berries. ♀

Aucuba japonica **'Pepper Pot'** Relatively compact, with small, even, distinct spots. ♂

Aucuba japonica **'Picturata'** Each leaf features a bright yellow central splash with speckles around the edge. ♂

Aucuba japonica **'Rozannie'** Broad, deep green leaves on a slow-growing plant. Self-fertile, but even more large red fruits are produced with the presence of a male plant. ☿ 6 ft. (2 m)

Aucuba japonica **'Salicifolia'** Slender, bright green leaves on blue-green stems; generous with its red fruits. ♀

Aucuba japonica **'Seven Hills'** Slow-growing, very hardy form with red berries. ♀

Aucuba japonica **'Variegata'** The original speckled form now outclassed by 'Gold Dust'. ♀

Colorful new cultivars with a wide range of patterns and leaf shapes have been arriving from Japan in recent years. Most have yet to be tested in different regions but some look promising. 'Akebono' has cream-colored young growth that matures to green. 'Ki Mi' has lightly gold-spotted foliage and yellow berries. 'Mangetsu' has ruffled green leaves speckled around the edge with creamy yellow centers—and the berries are striped! 'Ogon-no-tsuki' has narrow leaves with a bright flash of yellow in the center.

Berberis

Colorful and resilient, with no fear of invasion

Adaptable evergreen and deciduous shrubs in a range of sizes; all are spiny, occasionally dangerously so. Usually rather twiggy in habit, with distinctive yellow wood, the stringy branches of barberries are unexpectedly robust. The foliage varies from pale green, through bluish tones, to dark, glossy, or almost leaden green. Deciduous species often feature impressive autumn color. The neat symmetrical flowers, in yellow, gold, or orange tones, are gathered in the leaf joints in tight or more open clusters. Often, attractive fruits follow in a range of shades from coral to red to blue to black, sometimes changing color as they mature.

Height 3 to 12 ft. (1 to 3.6 m)
Hardiness Z6 or 7

To be clear, I'm not recommending Japanese barberry (*Berberis thunbergii*), which can be an invasive menace! But there are over 600 other barberry species, some of which are impressive and well-behaved garden plants. And a few of these are important, and sometimes surprising, options for the dry shade garden.

Berberis are sometimes considered rather charmless utilitarian shrubs, and it may be true that some are more valuable as low-maintenance plants for the wider landscape than as

The evergreen *Berberis darwinii*, with its small holly-like leaves, regularly produces an attractive crop of plum-blue berries, sometimes alongside a few late flowers.

One of the most colorful and elegant of spring shrubs is *Berberis* ×*stenophylla*. Its spiny branches also make it good choice for a boundary hedge, and it is never invasive.

colorful plants for the home garden. But the flowering display of *B. darwinii* and the almost all-year color changes in *B. wilsoniae* bring at least some species into the top rank of specimen shrubs. And evergreen barberries have the obvious attraction of foliage in winter, foliage that is usually presentable at least. As is often the case, evergreens predominate in my recommendations.

All barberries are spiny shrubs, some evergreen and some deciduous, and those discussed here are suitable for areas as cold as zone 6. The spines are, in fact, modified leaflets and are often carried in groups of three. In some species they are quite short, in two of those listed here they are much longer. While spines can be a virtue in boundary hedging in some situations, take care where you site those with the longest spines, which can penetrate the clothing of adults and the tender skin of young children. I never cite their spines as a reason not to plant barberries, but be sure to match the species to the situation. All require careful handling when planting or pruning; wear thick gloves that cover your wrists.

The barberries featured here are surprisingly resilient, with tough twiggy branches that make effective ground cover in those species with a spreading growth habit. The yellow or orange flowers are impressively displayed in clusters. The fruits are generously produced, with no special pollination requirements and they seem to be low on the list of priorities for hungry birds in winter. Many barberries may prove deer-resistant in your area, proving just how valuable these shrubs can be.

RECOMMENDED SELECTIONS

Berberis darwinii Has small, dark, glossy, evergreen leaves, which perfectly set off the open clusters of orange flowers and plum-colored berries. It is more often planted in sun but worth trying in milder areas. Discovered by Charles Darwin on the Beagle voyage. 6 to 12 ft. (2 to 3.6 m) Z7

Berberis julianae Famed for its vicious trios of 1½ in. (3.7 cm) spines. Relatively long, narrow, evergreen leaves are interspersed with generous clusters of lightly fragrant yellow flowers. The hardiest of the evergreens. 8 to 10 ft. (2.4 to 3 m) Z6

Berberis sanguinea (Berberis panlanensis) Long slender evergreen foliage and, again, 1½ in. (3.7 cm) spines, with crowded clusters of golden, sometimes greenish, flowers that give way to red berries, maturing to black. 6 to 9 ft. (2 to 2.7 m) Z7

Berberis ×stenophylla Classic evergreen boundary hedge plant that matures into a dense thicket of arching, fine but strong twigs. Slightly leaden green foliage is coupled with small but prolific golden flowers, then tiny bluish fruits. 8 to 10 ft. (2.4 to 3 m) Z6

Berberis verruculosa Noticeably rough brown twigs carry small, dark green evergreen leaves; small golden flowers are followed by black fruits. 4 to 6 ft. (1.2 to 2 m) Z6

Berberis wilsoniae Invaluable, elegant, dense, and deciduous, featuring sea green leaves, yellow flowers, coral berries, and coral and orange fall color. Every garden should have one. 3 to 4 ft. (1 to 1.2 m) Z6

Small-leaved, reliable evergreens

Familiar, neat evergreen shrubs, ranging in height from a few inches to many feet. The leaves may be rounded or relatively narrow and are held in opposite pairs on slender but strong shoots. In spring, clusters of small yellowish flowers are held in the shoot tips and upper leaf joints.

Two species are suitable for dry shade and both feature many named forms. The littleleaf boxwood, *Buxus microphylla,* has leaves no larger than ¾ in. (2 cm) long and generally makes relatively small plants—often not more than 4 ft. (1.2 m) high. There are only a few variegated forms. The common boxwood, *B. sempervirens,* has slightly larger leaves, up to 1¼ in. (3 cm) long, and may grow as tall as 15 ft. (5 m), although most of the boxwoods listed below are more restrained. There are some bright and attractive variegated cultivars. In North America, littleleaf boxwood is most popular, but in Britain the taller, more varied forms of *B. sempervirens* are widely grown, often clipped to create topiary or knot gardens.

**Height 1 to 15 ft. (30 cm to 4.5 m)
Hardiness Z4 to 6**

Boxwood, or simply box, is a familiar small-leaved evergreen with many uses in the garden. These are valuable plants, whether as foundation plantings, as topiary, as low or taller hedging, as specimens, or as focal features. Good for structure, good as a striking accent, good to mark boundaries and enclose planting areas; although no one would say they are exciting, boxwoods have a comfortable, dependable solidity. Boxwoods are generally resistant to deer damage, which is one of the reasons they are so often seen in American gardens.

In general, choose slow-growing types that may better tolerate difficult conditions; vigorous types will cast too much additional shade and draw too much moisture from the soil. True, there are variegated selections that are more colorful but in dry shade these may be less successful than plain green-leaved forms. In shade, boxwoods need all the chlorophyll they can get.

RECOMMENDED SELECTIONS

Buxus **'Chicagoland Green'** A hybrid of *B. sempervirens* with rounded habit and moderate growth; ideal for hedges and accents. Develops bronzed winter tints. 4 ft. (1.2 m) Z4

Buxus **'Green Velvet'** Compact, low-mounding plant with dark green foliage and inconspicuous fragrant flowers. 2 ft. (60 cm) Z5

Buxus microphylla **'Faulkner'** Dense, rounded plant with relatively large, frost-resistant, dark bluish green, glossy leaves. Very tolerant. 2 ft. (60 cm) Z6

Buxus microphylla **var.** *japonica* **'Green Beauty'** Rounded growth with neat, glossy leaves that develop purple winter tints. 4 ft. (1.2 m) Z6

Buxus sempervirens **'Aureovariegata'** One of the larger variegated types, but dense and bushy and easily clipped to

The neat, rounded habit of many boxwoods is a welcome contrast to the more informal habit of surrounding dry shade perennials.

a modest size. Slightly grayish leaves are edged in creamy yellow. 10 ft. (1.5 m) Z6

***Buxus sempervirens* 'Elegantissima'** Makes a dense dome. The small leaves, each edged in creamy white, are sometimes slightly misshapen but this does not affect the overall appearance of the plant. 5 ft. (1.5 m) Z6

***Buxus sempervirens* 'Graham Blandy'** Neat, upright habit but modest size; ideal as a vertical accent. 6 ft. (2 m) Z6

Neatly edged with white, the small, even leaves of *Buxus sempervirens* 'Aureovariegata' bring some valuable brightness to a shady spot.

The pale variegation of *Buxus sempervirens* 'Elegantissima' adds a splash of color to the border. It can be used as a specimen or as a low hedge, or clipped into geometric shapes.

Danae racemosa

Impressively drought-tolerant evergreen

An intriguing, unusually resilient plant that develops into a broad arching shrub as it matures. The branches are lined with dark, shining, pointed oval leaves up to 4 in. (10 cm) long. Strictly speaking, these leaves are actually flattened stems (phylloclades), but they function perfectly well as leaves. In early summer, clusters of up to six greenish yellow flowers open at the tips of the side shoots and are followed by bright red berries, maturing from green. *Danae* is related to *Ruscus*, but unlike *Ruscus* it has no spines and has both male and female parts in individual flowers, so a single plant can fruit prolifically. Unfortunately, this plant is not widely available in nurseries and garden centers because seed is slow to germinate, it will not root from cuttings, and young plants are slow to develop to a marketable size.

Height 3 ft. (1 m)
Hardiness Z6

D*ANAE RACEMOSA* is one of the most resilient shrubs you can grow. Although there are other choices that are more winter hardy, the ability of this shrub to thrive in almost any conditions (except dry soil in full sun) make it a valuable addition to the dry shade flora. Its growth somewhat resembles that of a short bamboo, the stems tending to

One of the most resilient of dry shade evergreens, *Danae racemosa* also makes unusually long-lasting cut foliage for indoor arrangements.

bow outwards as they grow. These stems are lined with deep, almost emerald-green leaves and the tips of the shoots sport small, open clusters of creamy early summer flowers. These are followed by little green berries that mature to bright red. It produces fruit more reliably than the closely related *Ruscus aculeatus* (Butcher's broom).

Dependable rather than flamboyant, Alexandrian laurel makes an appealing, ground-covering specimen or a good background for more colorful plants. This is also a splendid plant to cut for the vase in winter. Its glossy foliage lasts an extraordinarily long time and can be reused when the accompanying flowers have faded—sometimes more than once.

Euonymus

Reliable, well-behaved evergreens with attractive foliage

The *Euonymus* listed here are evergreen shrubs that vary in height from a few inches to over ten feet. The paired leaves are dark green and universally leathery in texture, but with a range of attractive variegations; depending on the cultivar, they can be as short as ½ in. (12 mm) or up to 3 in. (7.5 cm) long. Small greenish or yellowish flowers open in loose clusters in summer, but flowering—and maturity into colorful fruits—is far less consistent than in some of the deciduous species.

Height 6 in. to 12 ft. (15 cm to 3.6 m)

Hardiness Z5 or 6

OST *Euonymus* are deciduous (like the attractive but sometimes invasive *E. alatus*); the relatively few evergreen species are native mainly to shaded habitats, so they are among the most dependable of all dry shade stalwarts. With so many choices, make your selection based on personal preference, the growth habit you need for your

Euonymus range from dark green to this brilliantly colored *E. fortunei* 'Blondy' with its bold, golden-splashed foliage.

The rich green leaves of *Euonymus fortunei* 'Emerald Gaiety' are variably edged in white and become tinged with pink as the cold weather arrives.

situation, and the coloration that will create attractive associations with nearby plants.

Some euonymus stay low in a prostrate habit, creeping across the soil to make suberb ground cover. Some are much more neat and compact, ideal for small gardens and even containers in dry, shady sites. Some develop into effective specimen plants. Still others are strikingly vertical in growth; a few will climb and cling to walls, fences, and tree trunks—these are listed in the chapter on climbers.

Their foliage is quite leathery, but with an appealing range of white, cream, yellow, and gold variegations. This coloration may be edged, and can vary from a slender line to half the leaf width; it may be central, from a slim central tracing to a bold splash; speckling and spotting is seen in some cultivars; in a few, the foliage opens yellow then later greens up.

RECOMMENDED SELECTIONS

Euonymus fortunei Trailing, climbing or bushy shrub with neat elliptic leaves; good as edging, in containers, as ground cover, or as a vine. Considered invasive in a few areas. Z5

Euonymus fortunei 'Blondy' Deep green leaves, with a central creamy splash (gold in sun) that varies from a slender line or spreads out to dominate the leaf. Makes a stylish, rounded specimen plant. 18 in. (45 cm)

Euonymus fortunei 'Harlequin' Leaves unfurl almost pure white, maturing to green with white speckles. Delightful or hideous—depending on your point of view. Slow- and low-growing. 1 ft. (30 cm)

Euonymus fortunei 'Emerald Gaiety' Neat in growth, with an irregular white margin to the dark leaves that becomes pink tinted in winter. 3 ft. (1 m)

Euonymus fortunei 'Emerald 'n' Gold' Compact, dense plant in bright green, with a broad bright yellow margin becoming cream with pink tints in winter. Climbs effectively. Dramatic. 3 ft. (1 m)

Euonymus fortunei 'Emerald Surprise' Similar to 'Emerald

Gaiety' but with larger leaves that do not develop pink tinges in winter. Will climb. 3 ft. (1 m)

Euonymus fortunei **'Silver Queen'** Justifiably an old favorite; leaves are cream-edged in spring then become whiter with rosy winter tints. Unusually, produces good flowers and small orange-and-pink fruits. Probably the best climber. 8 ft. (2.4 m)

Euonymus fortunei **'Tustin'** Completely prostrate; makes an effective and efficient ground cover. Rich green leaves are brightly picked out with pale veins. 6 in. (15 cm)

Euonymus japonicus Substantial, dense, bushy shrub with dark, glossy foliage. Makes a good specimen plant or a hedge, and grows well by the ocean. Z6

Euonymus japonicus **'Bravo'** Small in stature, but large-leaved, with green foliage edged in cream and sometimes all-white shoot tip. 18 in. (45 cm)

Euonymus japonicus **'Chollipo'** Relatively upright plants with dark green leaves margined in cream. 12 ft. (3.6 m)

Euonymus japonicus **'Microphyllus Albovariegatus'** Dwarf, tight, rather upright plant with small dark leaves narrowly edged in white and tinted pink in winter. 3 ft. (1 m)

Euonymus japonicus **'Ovatus Aureus'** Slightly yellowish green leaves feature broad creamy markings, richer in sun, and most colorful on young growth. 5 ft. (1.5 m)

Euonymus japonicus **'Président Gauthier'** Spreading, large-leaved plant, each leaf with an irregular dark green center, white margin, and silvery green midzone. 3 ft. (1 m)

Euonymus kiautschovicus Less well-known, rather spreading shrub with an open habit and bright green foliage. Dependably produces pink and orange fruits. Z6

Euonymus kiautschovicus **'Manhattan'** Smaller and less vigorous than the species, and easier to train as a hedge or arch. 6 ft. (2 m)

There is quite a muddle between those cultivars of *Euonymus japonicus* whose names are in Latinate form. The result is that you may see the same plant under two different names—even at the same nursery. Here's the scoop.

'Aureopictus' is correctly 'Aureus'
'Aureovariegatus' is correctly 'Ovatus Aureus'
'Macrophyllus Albus' is correctly 'Latifolus Albomarginatus'
'Microphyllus Aureus' is correctly 'Microphyllus Pulchellus'
'Microphyllus Variegatus' is correctly 'Microphyllus Albovariegatus'
'Pulchellus Aureovariegatus' is correctly 'Microphyllus Aureovariegatus'

Got that?

Deciduous or evergreen, for foliage and fruits

A large group of deciduous and evergreen shrubs (and even trees) from a varied range of climates, hollies mature into a wide range of shapes and sizes. They are primarily grown for their foliage and/or berries. The leaves are usually untoothed, though often spiny, and the evergreens feature many different variegations while deciduous species may display fiery fall color. The small white flowers produced in late spring or early summer are followed by attractive—and often plentiful—fruit, most frequently in red but also sometimes in orange, yellow, black, or white. Male and female flowers are usually carried on separate plants, so related plants of both genders are required to ensure fruit is set.

Height 3 to 12 ft. (1 to 3.6 m)
Hardiness Z5 to 7

Hollies are colorful, dependable, and good for wildlife. Evergreen species are the best choices for dry shade because they can make the most of available light year round. Strangely, those that thrive in North America are much less successful and less widely grown in Britain—and vice versa. Dry shade favorites in North America include the American holly (*Ilex cornuta*) and Chinese holly (*I. opaca*), where they are best suited to the heat and humidity of the eastern US. These species are rarely seen in Britain where *I. aquifolium* is the most widely grown. Forms of both inkberry (*I. glabra*) and Yaupon holly (*I. vomitoria*) may also be suitable. It is worth working through the maze of different cultivars to find those that will thrive in your area and in your own dry shade garden.

So, what should you look for in dry shade hollies? The best possible combination of: manageable, evergreen growth that can easily be controlled by simple pruning (so, not too spiny); good berries or good foliage (or preferably both); tolerance of challenging dry shade conditions; and suitability for your climate. And it helps if there is good availability in local nurseries. Some of the selections listed here might seem a little tall, but you can cut their berried foliage for the house as winter decorations and, with careful pruning, the plants can be kept to a modest size while still maintaining a natural appearance.

RECOMMENDED SELECTIONS

Narrowing down the choices brings us to one native British species, one native American species, and one from Asia. All come in both female (♀) and male (♂) forms.

***Ilex aquifolium* (English holly)** Vastly variable, often combining colorful leaves and colorful fruits; the best choice in Britain. Also good in the Pacific Northwest but

The American holly, *Ilex opaca*, is an invaluable evergreen for American
gardens but is rarely grown in the unsuitable British climate

The very distinctive evergreen foliage of *Ilex cornuta* is brightened by the vivid sparks of its crimson berries.

increasingly considered invasive both there and in California. Z7

***Ilex aquifolium* 'Angustifolia'** Purple stems carry rather narrow leaves with slender spines. ♂ and ♀ forms. 3 ft. (1 m)

***Ilex aquifolium* 'Aurifodina' ('Muricata')** Flat, deep green leaves are edged yellow and mottled in yellowish green; bright red berries. Tall, but you can cut for indoor display. ♀ 10 ft. (3 m)

***Ilex aquifolium* 'Dude'** Broad yellow margins surround its relatively spine-free leaves, also features purple stems and is especially generous with its pollen. ♂ 6 ft. (2 m)

***Ilex aquifolium* 'Flavescens'** Leaves suffused in greenish yellow, red berries, and almost no spines. The better the light, the better the coloring. ♀ 8 ft. (2.4 m)

***Ilex aquifolium* 'Handsworth New Silver'** Purple young stems carry deep green, almost spine-free leaves mottled grey and edged in white; prolific red berries. Tall, but you can cut for arrangements. ♀ 10 ft. (3 m)

***Ilex aquifolium* 'Silverdust'** ('Ingramii' in the UK) Purple stems and new foliage, and dark spiny leaves speckled in white and grey tones. ♂ 10 ft. (3 m)

***Ilex cornuta* (Chinese holly)** A dense, rounded evergreen, sometimes wider than high, with glossy leaves and generous red berry production. Z7

***Ilex cornuta* 'Berries Jubilee'** Relatively large, glossy dark green leaves, and prolific bright red berries. ♀ 5ft. (1.5 m)

***Ilex cornuta* 'Dwarf Burford'** Dark glossy leaves with only one terminal spine and prolific in fruit. ♀ 6 ft. (2 m)

***Ilex cornuta* 'O. Spring'** Foliage is irregularly edged and blotched in yellow and grayish green. ♂ 6 ft. (2 m)

***Ilex opaca* (American holly)** The holly most similar to the European *I. aquifolium*, with prickly leaves and red berries. Hard to find in Britain. Z6, except as noted

***Ilex opaca* 'Christmas Snow'** Slow-growing, rather upright plants. Leaves have yellow margins with creamy mottling; red fruits. One of the hardiest hollies. ♀ 5 ft. (1.5 m) Z5

***Ilex opaca* 'Maryland Dwarf'** Low and spreading, with

olive-green leaves. Berries are red but not plentiful. ♀ 3 ft. (1 m)

Ilex opaca **'Miss Helen'** Short-spined olive green leaves and prolific red fruits. Does well in a range of climates. ♀ 10 ft. (3 m)

Ilex opaca **'Nelson West'** Compact male plant that can be used as a pollinator, with slender spiny leaves. ♂ 13 ft. (4 m)

Ilex opaca **'Stewart's Silver Crown'** Slow-growing plants. Leaves are mottled grey and have creamy margins; red fruits. ♀ 5 ft. (1.5 m)

Hollies with a neat marginal variegation sport interesting patterns, and the winter berries will draw birds to the garden.

Attractive evergreen with three seasons of interest

One of about seventy species of attractive and resilient evergreen shrubs in the genus *Mahonia*, related to *Berberis* but distinguished by their absence of thorns and by their leaves, which are up to 1 ft. (30 cm) long and pinnately divided like roses. *M. aquifolium* is a suckering shrub, but cultivars vary greatly in their growth habit. The shining green, spiny, hollylike leaflets often develop bronzed or reddish overtones in winter. In spring, generous clusters of rich yellow flowers, 3 to 4 in. (7 to 10 cm) across, open at the shoots' tips and in the upper leaf joints, often followed by blue-black berries. Some forms may actually be *M. ×wagneri*, which is a hybrid with the slightly bluish *M. pinnata*.

Height 3 ft. (1 m)
Hardiness Z5 or 6

ALTHOUGH sometimes viewed as a rather utilitarian plant, more functional than fantastic, some forms would be well worth growing even if they needed cosseting. But this is not a fussy plant. In fact, this valuable North American native grows naturally in much of the western and eastern US (although not in between), although it may be irritatingly weedy in some areas. Some of the more familiar cultivars, however, originate in Europe.

With lustrous foliage all year round, bright yellow spring flowers, deep blue summer and fall berries, and a tendency to develop volcanic tones in the foliage with the onset of cold weather, these are valuable shrubs. Cultivars vary from short and spreading at one extreme to taller and more upright, often becoming sparse at the base. Fortunately they tolerate pruning, but you can do the job by simply cutting the flowering or berried stems, or the winter foliage, for the house. Mahonias vary in their suckering capability too, some spreading helpfully and others remaining more compact.

Happy in most gardens, this mahonia is only unsuitable in chalky and other soils with a high pH, especially in full sun. Desiccating winds may also burn foliage in full sun but, in dry shade, just give them a little extra water and mulch to help them become established; with regular watering they will prove positively luxuriant.

RECOMMENDED SELECTIONS

Mahonia aquifolium Although the straight species is fine, there are other choice options, with blood from *M. pinnata* in some forms. Z6

Mahonia aquifolium 'Apollo' Vigorous but ground-hugging, the dense growth makes this an excellent ground cover. With its red-stalked leaves, tendency to reddish winter

The purplish foliage of many forms of *Mahonia aquifolium* sets off the clusters of
yellow buds. These soon open to neon yellow flowers followed by blue-black berries.

color, and fragrant golden yellow flowers this is probably the pick of the bunch. 2 ft. (60 cm)

Mahonia aquifolium **'Atropurpurea'** Reliably develops dark, reddish purple foliage in winter and spring. 3 ft. (1 m)

Mahonia aquifolium **'Compactum'** Sounds like an appealing form, and the true plant is. Sadly, a range of different forms is now sold under this name, some of them vigorous and upright. So best avoided.

Mahonia aquifolium **'King's Ransom'** Upright habit, with wine-red spring growth, bluish tints in summer, and bronze tones in winter. Probably a hybrid. 5 ft (1.5 m)

Mahonia aquifolium **'Smaragd'** Fairly compact and slightly spreading, unusually large clusters of flowers are carried all along the stems. Bronzed foliage in winter. 2 ft. (60 cm)

Mahonia ×wagneri **'Pinnacle'** A hybrid with *M. pinnata*, features vigorous and upright growth that carries reddish spring foliage maturing to a bright green color, which it retains through the winter months. 5 ft. (1.5 m) Z5

Ruscus aculeatus

Resilient and attractive—in the garden and in the vase

Once surprisingly assigned to the lily family, *Ruscus* now occupies a smaller family alongside *Aspidistra*, *Danae*, *Liriope*, and *Polygonatum*. All *Ruscus* species are small, similar evergreens whose leaves are reduced to tiny scales but whose short stems have modified into tough, sharply pointed structures called *phylloclades* that resemble leaves. In the most common butcher's broom, *R. aculeatus*, the green upright stems grow in a dense mass and are clad in 1 in. (2.5 cm) phylloclades with the texture of long-dried leather. The tiny flowers are carried on the surface of these "leaves"; red berries follow. Most plants are either male or female—both, of course, are needed to produce berries.

Height 30 in. (75 cm)
Hardiness Z7

THEY MAY BE unusual in the botanical sense, but these steadily spreading evergreen shrubs have the tough determination to thrive in dry and shady places. They never grow too tall and never invade other parts of the garden. But they are very tough, and they are also very green—even the stems are green. (It has been suggested that the

One of the most dependable shrubs for demanding conditions, *Ruscus aculeatus* not only features attractive evergreen foliage but also appealing marble-sized scarlet berries.

young shoots can be cooked and eaten like asparagus but I'm not convinced.) The only difficulty is that, usually, male and female flowers are carried on separate plants so plants of both sexes are required to ensure that the colorful berries are produced—but they can be produced prolifically, sparkling against those dark green "leaves."

Ruscus also make unusually long-lasting cut foliage, and the clumps are so dense that they can happily lose a few stems without their absence being obvious. The stems will even survive for ten days *out* of water. Like the closely related *Danae racemosa*, butcher's broom will often last through two or three changes of fresh flowers.

RECOMMENDED SELECTIONS

Ruscus aculeatus **Hermaphrodite Form** A number of plants with male and female parts in the same flower are grown under this name. They will fruit reliably. ☿

Ruscus aculeatus **'Christmas Berry'** A dependably dwarf form, with dark green foliage and a prolific crop of bright red berries. ☿ 18 in. (45 cm)

Ruscus aculeatus **'John Redmond'** Very dwarf, hermaphrodite form with dark red berries set against mid green foliage. ☿ 1 ft. (30 cm)

Ruscus aculeatus **'Wheeler's Variety'** A taller hermaphrodite form, which apparently comes true from seed. ☿ 18 in. (45 cm)

Ruscus hypoglossum Has larger leaves and also slightly larger berries than *R. aculeatus* but softer, paler foliage, which makes it more accommodating as cut material for arrangements. Unfortunately, no hermaphrodite forms are available, so you will need at least two plants.

Sarcococca

Powerfully fragrant winter evergreen

Sweetbox are small- to medium-sized evergreen shrubs related to boxwood. Some species slowly develop into thickets by steady suckering while others are more restrained. The usually upright stems, often unbranched until near the tips, are clothed in dark green, pointed, glossy, 2 to 3 in. (5 to 7.5 cm) leaves. In winter, the small male and female flowers appear alongside each other and in the leaf joints; they have no petals but exude a powerful fragrance. These little flowers are followed by very long-lasting berries in black, dark red, or purple. The variations are mainly in size, the color of the berries, and whether the plants produce suckers. That wonderful scent seems universal.

Height 18 in. to 6 ft. (45 cm to 2 m)
Hardiness Z5 to 8

DESPITE THEIR captivating winter fragrance, sweetbox flowers are relatively inconspicuous, so for the unsuspecting visitor the source of the scent can be perplexing. But sweetbox is also valued for its resilient evergreen foliage, which is a rich, lustrous green, sometimes with slightly lead-black overtones. The stems make fine additions to winter arrangements, hide one or two stems in a more colorful mixed bouquet to benefit from that wonderful scent.

Sarcococca hookeriana is one of the most valuable of evergreen shrubs, thanks to its neat, glossy leaves and tiny but highly fragrant winter flowers.

Sarcococca ruscifolia

Although some species spread dependably by short suckers they never overstep their bounds. The larger species may sometimes become irregular in shape, sending out long inelegant shoots. Simply cut them out, making the cut within the mass of the plant.

The unobtrusive, creamy or red-and-cream flowers, tucked into the leaf joints, are followed by berries that can last on the plant until the following year's flowers open, so blossoms and fruits may be carried on the plant together. The blue-black, deep purple, or bright cherry-red berries are eventually distributed by birds, and so easily transplantable seedlings may pop up around the garden.

Sweetbox thrives in the shade and is drought-tolerant once established. However, if it is too dry at flowering time, plants may not set fruit well. But this is just another reason to set up automatic irrigation.

RECOMMENDED SELECTIONS

Sarcococca confusa Slowly suckering, with cream flowers that give way to black berries. 6 ft. (2 m) Z6

Sarcococca hookeriana Suckers into thickets of unusually long foliage; white flowers then blue-black berries. 5 ft. (1.5 m) Z6

Sarcococca hookeriana. var. *digyna* Slimmer leaves than *S. hookeriana* and altogether more delicate-looking—but hardier. 5 ft. (1.5 m) Z5

Sarcococca hookeriana var. *digyna* 'Purple Stem' Has a purple tint to its young growth, with pinkish flowers. 5 ft. (1.5 m) Z5

Sarcococca hookeriana var. *humilis* The most dwarf sweetbox, spreads steadily by suckers; pink-tinged flowers are followed by blue-black berries. 18 in. (45 cm) Z6

Sarcococca ruscifolia Dense, bushy, and slow-growing; less hardy than other species. Creamy flowers are followed by red berries. 3 ft. (1 m) Z8

Sarcococca ruscifolia 'Dragon's Gate' Compact plant, with small foliage, cream flowers, and red berries. Also less hardy than most species. 2 ft. (60 cm) Z8

Symphoricarpos

Bursting with berries all winter long

Robust, adaptable, and very hardy deciduous shrubs that usually produce a thicket of slender wiry stems lined with small, sometimes grayish, leaves. Tiny white or pale pink, bell-shaped flowers are usually carried in clusters at the shoot tip and in the leaf joints and are surprisingly rich in nectar, making them popular with bees. These are followed by the chief glory of snowberry, the white, pink, speckled, or sometimes purplish, rather pulpy fruits, which remain in good condition for many months. Happy in a range of soils and conditions, some types spread consistently to make dense patches, others remain in tighter clumps.

Height 3 to 6 ft. (1 to 2 m)
Hardiness Z2 to 4

FOR AN UNFASHIONABLE shrub, the snowberry has some really good qualities. First, it is very hardy even down to zone 2 in some species; it will take winter temperatures of –0°F (–45°C) so few gardeners need worry that it will struggle to see spring. Adaptability and tolerance of a wide range of conditions are other valuable traits. In the dry

Symphoricarpos ×doorenbosii 'Amethyst' may have the tiniest of flowers but its long-lasting fall and winter fruits are attractive to birds and make a great addition to winter bouquets. Photo courtesy Proven Winners—www.provenwinners.com

garden, snowberry will thrive as a hedge or as a specimen plant and some species are also sufficiently dense and spreading to form ground cover. But the best garden shrubs offer some overpowering ornamental quality and with the snowberry the fruit take charge.

Although not large, snowberry fruits can be produced in such numbers that they weigh the shoots down to the ground. As the name implies, white is the most common color but the fruits may also be pink, occasionally purple or red, or white with pink speckles or a delicate pink flush. And they last for months, as the birds seem to ignore them— as spring approaches it may be winter wetness and the

The colorful, yellow edged foliage of *Symphoricarpus orbiculatus* 'Variegatus' is eye-catching in the shade border and its bright red berries earn it the common name 'coralberry'.

occasional mouse that finally brings the display to a close. Gardeners should avoid eating them, too, as they may cause a mildly upset stomach.

Most snowberries develop an arching habit, accentuated in fall by the weight of those prolific fruits. If the shrubs become ragged or untidy, fairly brutal spring pruning will rejuvenate them. However, in dry shade it pays to soak them occasionally during the first season after such heavy pruning to ensure that the tendency to resprout is not held back by drought.

RECOMMENDED SELECTIONS

Symphoricarpos albus **var.** *laevigatus* Vigorous, densely suckering plant laden with marblelike white berries. The most tolerant of all snowberries. 6 ft. (2 m) Z3

Symphoricarpos ×*doorenbosii* **'Amethyst'** Developed for cutting. Unusually well branched, with copious, bright, coral-pink berries that last well. 5 ft. (1.5 m) Z3

Symphoricarpos ×*doorenbosii* **'Magic Berry'** Smaller and neater than many, with rosy pink berries. 4 ft. (1.2 m) Z4

Symphoricarpos ×*doorenbosii* **'Mother of Pearl'** Relatively dwarf, with densely growing branches that are generously covered with blushed white berries. 4 ft. (1.2 m) Z4

Symphoricarpos ×*doorenbosii* **'White Hedge'** Compact, but rather upright in growth and vigorous, with small white berries in a generous crop. 4 ft. (1.2 m) Z4

Symphoricarpos orbiculatus Purplish pink berries, small, but produced very generously. 'Foliis Variegatis' has smaller, yellow-edged leaves that may revert to plain green. 6 ft. (2 m) Z2

The hardiest of yews, and among the most adaptable

Taxus ×*media* is the result of crossing the European yew, *T. baccata,* with its relation the Japanese yew, *T. cuspidata.* This hybrid was first created in Massachusetts in about 1900. The familiar flat, very dark green leaves about ½ to 1¼ in. (1.2 to 3 cm) long, with white midribs, are arranged in a flat plane along the branches. The branches are reddish and eventually develop peeling bark; the foliage may also develop reddish tinges in winter. Male and female floral parts are usually carried on separate plants, so both are needed to ensure production of the fleshy red fruits on the female. Note that every part of the yew plant is poisonous—except the red fleshy part of the fruit. More cultivars are grown in North America, where their hardiness is valued in many areas, than in Britain.

Height 4 to 20 ft. (1.2 to 6 m)
Hardiness Z4

MOST GARDENERS see little need to distinguish between one species of yew and another. They all seem fairly similar, and the size and habit of the plants are more important than the species to which they are assigned. As it happens, *Taxus* ×*media* brings together qualities from both its parents—the vigor of *T. baccata* with the additional hardiness of *T. cuspidata.* Many cultivars of varying size and habit are suited to dry and shady conditions. Of course, some of the large and vigorous forms create unhelpful additional drought and deeper shade, but those of more modest proportions are very useful. The cultivars listed below are probably the most suitable for a wide range of climates and garden situations, including dry shade. In warmest zones (7 and 8), small, neat, and spreading forms of *T. baccata* will often do well in dry shade; in zone 3, choose forms of *T. cuspidata.* Avoid cultivars of *T. canadensis* as they may develop brownish coloring in winter.

RECOMMENDED SELECTIONS

Some plants are male (♂), some are female (♀). Both are required for the females to produce fruits.

Taxus ×*media* **'Brownii'** Compact, slow-growing plant with a rather rounded habit. Good as a low hedge. ♂ 6 ft. (2 m)

Taxus ×*media* **'Dark Green Spreader'** Slow growing and spreading in habit, the pale young shoots mature to dark green, tolerate clipping well, and keep their richness in winter. ♀ 4 ft. (1.2 m)

Taxus ×*media* **'Densiformis'** Slow growing, spreading habit and can be pruned regularly to create a low hedge. Fruits well. ♀ 3 ft. (1 m)

Taxus ×*media* **'Everlow'** Like a hardier version of the well known *T. baccata* 'Repandens' with low, widely spreading branches. ♀ 3 ft. (1 m)

This hybrid yew, *Taxus ×media* 'Dark Green Spreader', will provide dependable, evergreen foliage in the toughest conditions.

Taxus ×*media* **'Hicksii'** The most widely grown, upright growth, vigorous and good for garden hedges under a high canopy with prolific fruiting. ♀ 10 ft. (3 m)

Taxus ×*media* **'Margarita'** Limey new growth matures to dark green but brings light to shady areas. Upright habit, can be kept quite small by thoughtful pruning. ♀ 4 ft. (1.2 m)

Euonymus fortunei 'Silver Queen'

Bright and white self-clinging evergreen

This self-clinging vine resembles a variegated ivy in its overall appearance. Its oval, slightly toothed, rather leathery 2.5 in. (6 cm) evergreen leaves unfurl the color of the rich, thick country cream we're not allowed to eat any more, and then mature to slightly silvery green with an irregular creamy white border that may develop pink tints in winter. The almost white stems produce aerial roots that cling to rough surfaces. This form also reliably produces small greenish white flowers in summer and these may be followed by open clusters of orange-and-pink fruits.

Height 6 to 20 ft. (2 to 6 m)
Hardiness Z5

PREVIOUS Clinging to tree trunks by the rootlets on its stems, *Schizophragma hydrangeoides* 'Moonlight' features white lacecap flower heads, red stems, and silver-green leaves.

WE MAY TEND to think of evergreen euonymus as neat bushes or spreading ground cover, but a few climb remarkably well. Plant *Euonymus fortunei* 'Silver Queen' against any vertical surface and it will start to climb much like ivy, producing short clinging roots where the stems touch the hard surface. On rough surfaces, they take hold, while on smooth surfaces, rough winds and rain dislodge them. Climbers that need no assistance to cling to walls are always appreciated, and one that works well as an alternative to ivy will always be popular. Beware of the plain green-leaved forms, such as 'Coloratus' or 'Vegetus', which may prove too vigorous for some situations and their self-sown seedlings can become a nuisance and may spread into the wild.

'Silver Queen' has been known to reach 20 ft. (6 m), although 6 to 8 ft. (2 to 2.4 m) is more common especially in drier situations. Its overall bright coloring is invaluable on a wall, fence, or even a tree trunk in shady situations and combined with its tolerance of drought provides a welcome evergreen option. 'Emerald 'n' Gold' and any of the more vigorous variegated forms of *E. fortunei* are also worth a try.

The bright evergreen variegation of *Euonymus fortunei* 'Silver Queen' will light up dark spaces as it climbs tree trunks or walls, clinging by its aerial roots.

×*Fatshedera lizei* 'Annemieke'

Glowing, large-leaved, evergreen vine

A variegated form of a valuable hybrid between *Fatsia japonica* and *Hedera hibernica*. Tall, fat, upright, sometimes rusty-colored stems are rather lax in habit and produce no aerial roots (short roots on the underside of the stems). They carry shiny, five-lobed evergreen leaves 4 to 10 in. (10 to 20 cm) across and almost as long. Opening pale green with a generous pale yellow splash, as they mature they become rich, dark green with an irregular pale green stain seeping well into each lobe. In fall, small clusters of creamy flowers may be produced, unless prevented by frost, but the flowers are not followed by berries.

Height 6 ft. (1.8 m)
Hardiness Z8

THIS INTRIGUING hybrid brings together the qualities of ivy and what is sometimes called Japanese aralia in a valuable and subtly colorful combination. As you might guess, it neither develops into a self supporting shrub nor into a self-clinging climber but its long stout shoots are easy to tie in to a shady wall or fence. The foliage is a feature in itself and, as it develops a soft glow rather than a bright light, it makes a harmonious background for other plants.

In dry and shady situations it will certainly appreciate supplementary moisture; the size of the leaves and the length of stems between the leaves will be reduced in dry conditions and the plant will take longer to grow into its space.

Tree ivy sometimes flowers, but the plant is sterile so it produces no berries or seed to concern cautious gardeners worried that it might prove invasive. Indeed the one problem with this lovely vine is that it is much less hardy than ivy, so will not survive in colder gardens. Note that you may find it grown under the following names: 'Anna Mikkels', 'Aureomaculata', 'Lemon and Lime', and 'Maculata'. The more subtle variegation of ×*Fatshedera lizei* 'Variegata' consists of a fine white edge to the leaf. The plain green-leaved form makes a bold green background.

×*Fatshedera lizei* 'Annamieke' is a prettily variegated hybrid between *Fatsia* and *Hedera* that flowers but does not produce fruits.

Fine vines for dry and shady walls—if chosen carefully

Generally vigorous, evergreen, self-clinging climbers that thrive in shady situations. Although invaluable as ground cover, it is as vines that ivies have their place in the forest eco-system. Each slender woody stem is lined with short roots on the under-side (called aerial roots) and these grip tightly into bark, stonework, or even smooth surfaces. Rate of growth and eventual size depends largely on climate—and the height of the tree or wall being climbed. The evergreen foliage turns so that the blades of the leaves face the light, in many forms creating a dense cover. The leaves range in size from 1 to 12 in. (2.5 to 30 cm) and boast a vast number of shapes and patterns, many variegated.

Height 12 to 15 ft. (3.6 to 4.5 m)
Hardiness Z5–10

IN THE WILD, ivies root in the dry shade at the base of trees and use their aerial roots to cling to the bark as they climb. As they reach the top and emerge into more light, their pattern of growth changes; it becomes more compact and bushy, leaves become narrower and without lobes, and flowers and then fruits develop. It is these fruits, eaten by birds, that account for the sometimes unwelcome spread of ivies.

For this reason it is unwise to grow *Hedera hibernica*, the most invasive species, on walls and fences as it can produce fruits in just a few years. The large-leaved variegated forms of *H. algeriensis*, however, can be both impressively colorful and less likely to fruit—partly because they are more tender. Green-leaved forms of *H. helix* should probably also be avoided although many variegated forms fail to flower, so they are safe. Two forms of *H. helix* I would suggest as climbers are 'Ceridwen', in gold and green, and 'Glacier' in silver-grey and cream.

RECOMMENDED SELECTIONS

Hedera algeriensis **'Gloire de Marengo'** Dark green leaves open with creamy edges then maturing to grey and silvery grey at the edge. Dramatic and colorful. Z7

Hedera algeriensis **'Marginomaculata'** Pink leaf stems hold rounded foliage very densely speckled in sharp cream; develops pink tinges in winter. Z7

The three-lobed foliage of *Hedera helix* 'Ceridwen' is mainly variegated but there is a consistent minority of all-gold leaves.

Superlative self-clinging flowering vine

A vigorous deciduous climber, that clings to tree bark, walls, and other rough surfaces using aerial roots in the same way as ivy. The large, rich, deep green leaves are fairly rounded, slightly toothed, pointed at the tip, up to 4½ in. (12 cm) wide, and with paler undersides. As the stems mature, they develop attractive peeling brown bark. In early summer, the white lace-cap flower heads open; they are up to 10 in. (25 cm) across and may remain on the plant for many weeks after fading. On mature plants the effect can be dramatic.

Height 50 ft. (15 m) or more
Hardiness Z4

ONE OF OUR most impressive vines; a mature specimen cloaking a shady wall or clothing a bare tree trunk can be a dramatic sight. Climbing quickly once established, this vine roots naturally at the foot of tree trunks—which is of course generally a dry and shady place.

When planting climbing hydrangea at the base of mature trees, it is often easiest to dig a hole between the buttress roots and make a planting pocket of fresh new soil. Young plants can be slow to make good growth and their stems may need encouragement to take hold on their host bark or wall. Guide the growing shoots in the right direction, hold them in place with a cane, and tape the shoots to the wall using duct tape until their grip is reliable.

This climber can reach the top of mature trees, startling visitors by flowering 50 ft. (15 m) or more above ground. Its presence does very little harm to its host. Shady walls are covered very efficiently and if the short flowering side shoots grow inconveniently long, cut them back in spring. This trimming will remove the flower buds so either miss a year's flowering or cut back a third of the shoots each year to ensure that the overall flowering effect is not dramatically reduced.

RECOMMENDED SELECTIONS

Hydrangea anomala subsp. *petiolaris* **'Firefly'** Foliage softly margined in limey yellow that fades to green by late summer. 50 ft. (15 m)

Hydrangea anomala subsp. *petiolaris* **'Semiola'** Semi-evergreen hybrid with foliage lasting into the winter and even more impressive flowers. 60 ft. (18 m) or more

Hydrangea anomala subsp. *petiolaris* **'Mirranda'** Foliage boldly edged in gold; less vigorous and less boldly colored in shade than in sun. 50 ft. (15 m) or more

With its self-clinging roots, glowing foliage, and white summer lacecaps, *Hydrangea anomala* subsp. *petiolaris* 'Mirranda' can cover tree trunks, walls, and fences with color.

Vivid, dependable, and colorful self-clinger

Vigorous, self-clinging, deciduous vine that attaches itself to bark, brick, stone, or wood with tiny rounded suckers on the tips of its tendrils. The rather variable foliage, up to 8 in. (20 cm) long, tends to be a vivid bright green in spring then turns scarlet and purple in autumn. Each leaf is divided into three lobes or three distinct leaflets. In fall, the leaf blades sometimes drop off before the leaf stalks. The flowers are inconspicuous but give way to dark blue fruits. Similar to *P. quinquefolia*, Virginia creeper, with five leaflets, but with glossier foliage and a greater resilience in difficult situations.

Height 70 ft. (20 m)
Hardiness Z4

THIS PLANT is so easy, vigorous, and dependable that it scares some people. "Vigorous" is the part that worries them. But for tall trees with bare trunks this is a stupendous plant, doing exactly what it does in its native Asia—rooting at the base of the tree and climbing the trunk. Its glossy foliage shines in the dark and, in fall, the trunk is transformed into a vast fiery flame.

Known as Boston ivy from its ubiquity in the Massachusetts capital (no, not Boston in Lincolnshire) where it clothes the Harvard colleges, seeing it heading for the gutters makes one thing clear: You should plant it on a tree, where it can just climb and climb, or on a much lower wall or fence where

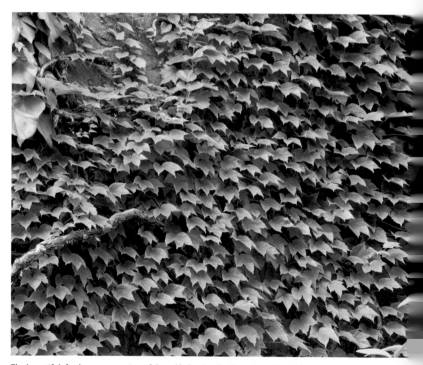

The beautiful, fresh green covering of the self-clinging *Parthenocissus tricuspidata* is a bright background for perennials, and sheds water away from the wall.

Although the small blue berries of *Parthenocissus tricuspidata* tend to be hidden by the fall foliage, the brilliant coloring of these leaves is invaluable.

you can reach it on a short ladder to keep it in bounds. Do not plant it on a house wall where cutting it back to keep it out of the gutters and off the roof will be impossible.

The straight species is superb, but try the forms listed below as well. Surprisingly, Boston ivy can also be grown on the flat as ground cover. Plant it in the less dry and less shady place and guide its growth into the drier, shadier area.

RECOMMENDED SELECTIONS

Parthenocissus tricuspidata **'Beverley Brooks'** Purple foliage in summer that turns bright red in fall.

Parthenocissus tricuspidata **'Fenway Park'** Chartreuse yellow foliage in sun but pale yellowish green in shade and valuable for that. Found in Boston by by an arborist at the Arnold Arboretum walking to the Red Sox baseball stadium of this name.

Parthenocissus tricuspidata **'Lowii'** Features relatively small, slightly crimpled foliage and even more spectacular autumn color.

Parthenocissus tricuspidata **'Veitchii'** Has smaller foliage that is purple when young.

The boldest and most architectural of perennials

This imposing perennial has stout, deep roots that carry large, bold, more or less rounded, shallowly lobed, often evergreen leaves about 3 ft. (1 m) long, sometimes longer. Each arching leaf is glossy dark green and, unlike some *Acanthus* species, the leaves are not spiny. In summer, impressive spikes of flowers surge through the foliage; each two-lipped bloom is pinkish white and emerges colorfully from beneath a green hood. The flowers are followed by fat fruits like marbles that mature from green to brown.

Height 4 to 5 ft. (1.2 to 1.5 m)
Hardiness Z7

PREVIOUS The contrasting form and texture and color of *Heuchera* 'Chocolate Ruffles' and *Arum italicum* makes a dramatic foliage combination.

IN MORE luxurious conditions this dramatic perennial can be a nuisance, spreading aggressively and elbowing aside its neighbors. But sited in the more spartan dry shade, it behaves with commendable restraint. This form, with foliage significantly broader than the usual forms of *A. mollis*, is more suited to dry shade because that broader expense of leaf ensures that the plant makes the best of whatever light is available. The downside is that when powdery mildew strikes, there is more leaf to attack. And in dry shade mildew is more of a problem than in damp situations.

This is a multi-season plant, with luxurious foliage—especially in late spring and early summer—bold towers of flowers, and then interesting ornamental seed pods. Some gardeners remove these spent flower spikes, as the drain of energy into the ripening seeds can lead the foliage to become ragged.

Choose a site sheltered from strong winds, which may break the large leaves. Hail can also be damaging, but shade trees provide shelter. But think carefully before finally deciding where to plant this, or any acanthus. If you change your mind and decide to move the plant, some of those deep roots will be left in the soil, especially among tree roots where they are difficult to dig out. After your plant is happily settled somewhere else, those roots will sprout and in a year or two your original plant will have "returned."

RECOMMENDED SELECTION

***Acanthus mollis* Latifolius Group 'Rue Ledan'** Attractive form with pure white flowers.

The broad glossy leaves of *Acanthus mollis* Latifolius Group thrive
under the overhanging branches of *Parrotia persica*.

Splendid foliage plants in an increasing variety

Tuberous perennials, these two arum species—one summer-dormant and one winter-dormant—have bold, glossy, heart- or arrowhead-shaped leaves that are patterned in silver, spotted in black, or occasionally marked yellow. The typical arum family flowers are held upright in spring or summer: they consist of a cowl-like spathe usually in pale green or cream, sometimes with purplish tints, surrounding an upright spadix, usually in purple or cream. The flowers are followed by tightly packed upright clusters of red or orange fruits, much loved by birds.

Height 1 to 2 ft. (30 to 60 cm)
Hardiness Z4

In late summer, *Arum italicum* develops crowded heads of bright orange-red fruits that persist after the foliage has faded.

S TROLLING ROUND the Royal Horticultural Society's garden at Wisley near London, it is illuminating to see so many *Arum italicum* plants thriving happily around the base of beech hedges. And walking through the native woods not far away, there is *A. maculatum* growing happily under mature and stately beech trees. Their happy persistence in such difficult circumstances rightly indicates their suitability for dry shade. Nonetheless, if you have poor soil, dig a hole and fill it with good soil into which to plant.

Once these arums are established you will probably find that plants derived from bird-dropped seeds spring up in other parts of the garden. In a few parts of North America there is concern that *A. italicum* is spreading from gardens into natural areas.

RECOMMENDED SELECTIONS

Arum italicum Generally has relatively pointed, arrowhead-shaped, white-veined leaves that emerge in fall and die away in late spring. Creamy flowers appear during the leaves' last days. 'Marmoratum' has especially brightly marked leaves. Also look for 'Chameleon' and 'White Winter'. 12 to 14 in. (30 to 35 cm)

Arum maculatum Has broad green leaves, often spotted in black, which emerge in late winter; spring brings greenish spathes surrounding a purple spadix. 15 to 24 in. (38 to 60 cm)

The brightly marked foliage of *Arum italicum* 'Marmoratum' emerges around the time that leaves start to fall, and it lasts until spring, even under snow cover.

One of the most tolerant perennials for deep shade

From the steadily spreading roots, the glossy, rather leathery and tough, often very deep green leaves arise individually on long winged stalks, overlapping with each other to produce a steadily expanding clump. Each leaf is more or less elliptical in outline and in some forms may reach 30 in. (75 cm) in length, though 15 to 18 in. (38 to 45 cm) is more typical. Some forms are plain green, but the many variegated ones have the most appeal. The flowers are just ¾ to 1¼ in. (2 to 3 cm), cream outside and maroon within—but they are often unnoticed because they are carried on the root at ground level.

Height 18 in. to 3 ft. (45 cm to 90 cm)
Hardiness Z7 or 8

'Milky Way' is one of an increasing number of variegated aspidistras, many of which originate in Japan.

O FTEN RELEGATED to the darkest and least hospitable corner of the Victorian drawing room, and growing (or at least not dying) in the murkiest recesses of town houses, outside in the garden the aspidistra is transformed. Even in the dry shade garden it slowly develops into attractive glossy clumps of overlapping evergreen foliage making a very respectable ground cover. But the spread is always steady rather than aggressive—there are no concerns about less robust plants being smothered.

Aspidistras are not the hardiest of perennials, but even if the foliage is killed in winter it often grows freshly in spring. And in cold areas, variegated aspidistras are ideal planted in summer containers where they can enliven dull, shady corners where the soil is irredeemable—or genuinely non-existent.

In recent years the number of variegated forms has increased impressively, providing gardeners with choices that can set off sparks in shady borders. Streaked forms, spotted forms, and striped forms have joined the surprisingly appealing straight species and other non-variegated forms. Although these variegated forms are the most colorful, those most heavily marked may prove too slow and lack the necessary robustness to survive in dry shade. These variegated forms may also occasionally produce green leaves; if so, simply cut them out.

RECOMMENDED SELECTIONS

Aspidistra elatior **'Asahi'** The long, dark leaves up to 20 in. (50 cm) long become increasingly white towards the tips. 2 ft. (60 cm) Z7

Aspidistra elatior **'Milky Way'** Leaves are 15 in. (38 cm) long, spotted and striped with cream. 18 in. (45 cm) Z8

Aspidistra elatior **'Variegata'** A mix of both slender and broad white stripes run the whole length of the 30 in. (75 cm) leaves. 3 ft. (1 m) Z7

Although *Aspidistra elatior*, the cast-iron plant, is sometimes thought of as a
houseplant for dingy rooms, it also copes well with deep shade in the garden.

More valuable than the common name suggests

Low, mainly evergreen perennials grown both for foliage and flowers. The large, rounded, leathery, often glossy leaves may be up to 14 in. (35 cm) long; they rise on short stems from a stout, slow, but relentlessly spreading woody rhizome. In some forms, growth is tight and compact, in others the rhizomes are more vigorous and the leaves less crowded. Many bergenias develop purple or red tones to the foliage, especially in winter, and in some this is their main feature. Some forms develop more pronounced color in relatively dry conditions, but color less well in shade. In spring, fleshy, generally upright stems carry branched sprays of more or less bell-shaped, sometimes flared, red, purplish, pink, or white flowers.

Height 9 to 20 in. (23 to 50 cm)
Hardiness Z3 to 6

BERGENIAS have two of the most valuable resources to help plants thrive in dry shade: broad, evergreen foliage and a fat woody root system. Those leaves soak up every speck of light, and both the foliage and the rhizomes provide valuable moisture storage.

All bergenias usually flower well, though in some (not recommended here) the flowers may be hidden amid the leaves—*Bergenia* ×*schmidtii* is an example. They may also produce fewer flowers as the soil becomes increasingly impoverished. Although those in sunnier spots may be susceptible to spring frost, shade provides protection.

But bergenias vary. Avoid deciduous forms like *B. ciliata*

The bright white flowers of *Bergenia stracheyi* Alba Group are especially prolific, and the plant tolerates late spring frosts.

Bergenia 'Eric Smith' brings an invaluable combination
of bronzy winter foliage and welcome spring flowers.

as they are unable to capitalize on winter light. Avoid variegated and yellow-leaved forms like *B. cordifolia* 'Tubby Andrews' and *B. cordifolia* 'Lunar Glow', which are inherently less vigorous. Some, like 'Abendglut' and 'Bressingham Ruby' tend to develop a more open habit and this will be overencouraged in dry shade, leading to a sparse appearance.

Instead choose those bergenias that are evergreen and naturally tight in growth but with good-sized leaves. And keep in mind that foliage color provides an invaluable winter feature—even if its intensity may be muted by the lack of direct sunlight.

RECOMMENDED SELECTIONS

Bergenia **'Eric Smith'** Brilliant beetroot red winter foliage, which is distinctively puckered; cerise spring flowers. 12 to 16 in. (30 to 40 cm) Z4

Bergenia **'Eroica'** In winter, the undersides of the leaves are burgundy; in spring, red buds open to purple-pink flowers. 16 to 20 in. (40 to 50 cm) Z3

Bergenia **'Overture'** Purple-red winter color and deep red, bell-shaped spring flowers on neat plants. Similar to 'Eroica', but shorter. 12 to 16 in. (30 to 40 cm) Z5

Bergenia stracheyi **Alba Group** Very neat and compact plant, with reddish winter color on some plants and pink buds that open to white spring flowers. 12 to 14 in. (30 to 35 cm) Z6

Bergenia **'Rosi Klose'** Green winter foliage, with just a few red tints, but brilliant rose-pink spring flowers. 12 to 14 in. (30 to 35 cm) Z5

Brunnera macrophylla

Bright leaves, clouds of dainty spring flowers

The hairy, upright stems on the slowly spreading black roots of this tough deciduous perennial carry rough, more or less heart-shaped leaves up to 6 in. (15 cm) across. The leaves may be plain, fresh green, variegated in a few slower growing forms, or silvered to a greater or lesser degree. In spring, clouds of small, blue or sometimes white forget-me-not flowers appear. Siberian bugloss makes a dependable smothering cover that is also more reliably deer-resistant than most perennials. The natural wild species is an attractive plant; the many selected forms add extra style.

Height 12 to 18 in. (30 to 45 cm)
Hardiness Z3

THIS TOUGH, very cold hardy, and adaptable perennial is one of the most valuable for dry shade. It spreads steadily but is never invasive, and develops a good weed-smothering cover of overlapping foliage. In recent years this foliage has become a great deal more interesting. Older forms were typically plain green, sometimes with a scattering of

With a delicate appearance that belies its toughness, *Brunnera macrophylla* has pretty forget-me-not sprays just as the flowers of *Helleborus foetidus* are going to seed.

Adaptable and resilient, the wild green-leaved form of *Brunnera macrophylla* is one of the most dependable of dry shade perennials. Each spring, without fail, it produces pretty bunches of sky blue blooms.

silver spots. Now, we have an increasing range of brightly silvered forms, some with gold tints as well.

These forms are especially valuable because the variegated forms, like the dramatic 'Hadspen Cream', lack the vigor needed to survive in dry shade. ('Hadspen Cream' also has a habit of reverting to plain green.) It is true that the highly silvered forms luxuriate more visibly in richer conditions, and may be slower in dry shade. The sprays of small flowers are usually blue, but white-flowered forms lighten the shade even more. Look for more new forms as they become available, including newcomers with bicolored blue-and-white flowers.

Siberian bugloss are also good plants for shaded containers tended by absent-minded, or simply absent, gardeners. A few missed waterings will not kill a *Brunnera*.

RECOMMENDED SELECTIONS

Brunnera macrophylla Plain green leaves decorated with a few silvery spots, with clouds of tiny blue flowers. This is the most familiar form.

Brunnera macrophylla **'Betty Bowring'** Similar to the plain species, slightly silver-spotted leaves and clouds of clean white flowers.

Brunnera macrophylla **'Emerald Mist'** Green foliage that is boldly marked with a regular silver pattern, and blue flowers. The best compromise between leaf color and robustness for dry shade.

Brunnera macrophylla **'Jack Frost'** Very elegant, with green-veined silver foliage. A good choice for containers.

Brunnera macrophylla **'Kings Ransom'** Its silver foliage, green veins, and gold tints look promising, but the gold edges tend to turn brown in dry situations.

Brunnera macrophylla **'Langtrees'** Green leaves with a neat pattern of small silver spots.

Brunnera macrophylla **'Looking Glass'** Each leaf is entirely silver, very bright.

Brunnera macrophylla **'Mr Morse'** Silvery green-veined foliage, like that of the better known 'Jack Frost', but with white flowers.

The silvered foliage of *Brunnera macrophylla* 'Jack Frost' sets off the dainty light blue flowers and is also efficient at smothering weeds.

Elegance and resilience personified

Sedges are grasslike plants that make tight clumps or spread from the roots, sometimes vigorously. They vary in size from a few inches to over 4 ft. (1.2 m) and most are grown for their foliage, which varies from wispy and thread-like to almost sword-shaped, and there are attractive variegated and colored-leaved forms. Colors include rich green, pale green, various yellow and gold shades, and some popular bronze and brownish tones; the white- and yellow-variegated forms can be very colorful. Some feature attractive flowers held on distinctive triangular stems. Unfortunately, most sedges appreciate damp conditions so relatively few are suitable for dry shade; the most reliable choices are listed here.

Height 16 in. to 3 ft. (40 cm to 90 cm)
Hardiness Z5 to 8

S EDGES HAVE become increasingly popular in recent years and one reason is their versatility. It is not that all sedges will grow everywhere, but there are choices for every situation—including dry shade. Those that thrive in dry shade fall into two groups. Some grow in dry shade in their native habitats so are ideally suited to these trying conditions; others, while usually seen in less taxing conditions, can adapt to the extra stress. There are also a few sedges whose aggressiveness creates problems in most conditions but that are curtailed in dry shade.

Some of the most popular sedges feature foliage in rusty, brown, or bronze shades. While certainly appealing, these

Variegated sedges, like this old favorite *Carex oshimensis* 'Evergold', bring the best combination of color and robustness to dry shady conditions.

The more recently introduced *Carex* 'Ice Dance' also features spikes of brown-tipped summer flowers among its cream-edged leaves.

Two clump-forming American natives that grow naturally in dry and shady situations are *Carex appalachica*, which even grows under conifers, and *C. pensylvanica*; both have slender green leaves and early flowers.

tones are often far less effective in shade than in sunnier spots. Variegated forms can be especially impressive, along with the almost statuesque *Carex pendula*, and although some of the yellow- and gold-leaved forms may lose their bright coloring they still provide a welcome variation on green. Be aware that the leaves of some sedges can be sharp-edged, so wear gloves if you are tidying up or cutting back the plants

RECOMMENDED SELECTIONS

Carex **'Ice Dance'** Creeping steadily, dark green leaves are edged in creamy white. In dry shade, its normal vigor is restrained. 16 in. (40 cm) Z5

Carex morrowii **'Fisher's Form'** **('Goldband')** Leaf edges are cream at first, then whiter. 'Variegata' covers many other variegated forms, mainly edged in greenish-white. 16 in. (40 cm) Z5

Carex muskingumensis Pale green leaves radiate from the tops of stems like miniature palms. 'Oehme' has leaves edged in gold. 24 in. (60 cm) Z5

Carex oshimensis **'Evergold'** Shade brings out the best coloring of the central yellowish leaf stripe. 20 in. (50 cm) Z6

Carex pendula Tall, bold, clump-forming specimen with dark leaves and attractive drooping grayish tassels. 2 to 4 ft. (60 cm to 1.2 m) Z5

Carex phyllocephala **'Sparkler'** White-edged leaves radiate from the tops of short stems. Benefits from an occasional watering. 20 in. (50 cm) Z8

Corydalis

Easy evergreens with a long flowering season

The two species featured here are both clump-forming plants with repeatedly branched, rather succulent stems, carrying pretty, pale green leaves divided and then divided again into oval leaflets. Unlike many other *Corydalis* species, the plants do not form tubers. For a long period in spring and summer, each stem carries clusters of up to about 16 white or yellow flowers held just above the foliage, each bloom having two lips and a spur. These are followed by capsules of small black seeds, which are distributed by ants—hence the appearance of seedlings in cracks in walls.

Height 12 to 16 in. (30 to 40 cm)
Hardiness Z5 or 6

THESE ARE plants that turn up in all sorts of odd places. Attracted to the nutritious waxy appendage on every seed, ants will carry them off, stash them away, and so ensure that seedlings appear in walls, in chinks in fences, in the crotches of trees, and in other relatively inhospitable places. So although they require deliberate planting in the unfriendly territory of dry shade, they may spread from there to some surprising locations.

There are about 300 species of *Corydalis* but two stand out for dry shade. (Some botanists transfer these two plants into their own genus as *Pseudofumaria alba* and *Pseudofumaria lutea*.) Gardeners differ in their commitment to one or the

Ants left the seed of *Corydalis lutea* in a dry crack in the brickwork and it has developed into an attractive little plant despite being overhung by a cypress.

Corydalis ochroleuca, growing here in dry a rock crevice overhung by trees, sports lacy foliage and dainty drooping blooms.

other species; I have seen both do well. In areas where there is good light for at least two months in spring and where there is some spring moisture, perhaps under a tall deciduous tree canopy, you can also try the many colorful forms of *C. solida*.

Corydalis are especially valuable tucked into the base of dry shade shrubs and peeping out from under conifers. They are also attractive cascading down the bricks, logs, or boards on retaining walls and raised beds.

RECOMMENDED SELECTIONS

Corydalis lutea From midspring to early fall, bright yellow flowers are set against fresh green foliage. May self-seed freely. 12 to 16 in. (30 to 40 cm) Z6

Corydalis ochroleuca Sports white flowers with yellow tips from late spring until late summer. Self-seeds less than *C. lutea*. 12 to 14 in. (30 to 35cm) Z5

Dryopteris

A classic combination of toughness and lacy elegance

Evergreen, wintergreen, and deciduous ferns, *Dryopteris* are among the most tolerant of all ferns. The common name derives from the appreciation that this is a far more robust plant than the superficially similar but more delicate-looking *Athyrium filix-femina*, the lady fern. Having been originally applied solely to *D. filix-mas* the name "male fern" is now often applied to the whole genus. All male ferns are striking from early in the season when the fiddleheads, augmented by coppery scales, begin to uncurl. The fronds may be erect or more arching, narrowly lance-shaped or more oval, and regularly divided once or twice into smaller leaflets. The plants are generally well-behaved, the fronds arising from a slowly expanding central crown. Some species boast a large number of variants that may feature difficult Latinate cultivar names. In general, avoid forms that are small and slow growing in favor of more vigorous types.

Height 2 to 3 ft. (60 cm to 1 m)
Hardiness Z3 to 6

GARDENERS tend to assume that ferns require shade and moisture. But although that may be true of many, probably most, some ferns are far more tolerant. Step forward the male ferns, among the finest dry shade perennials. While as many as 350 species grow in a wide variety of situations around the northern hemisphere, the species listed here

Fortunately, there are many forms of *Dryopteris filix-mas*, the most tolerant of all ferns, so you can grow a range with different frond shapes and patterns.

have adapted to dry shade and proven so very variable that there are more than enough choices.

As well as a vast range of elegant laciness in the form of their fronds, male ferns feature delightful unfurling crosiers, sometimes in red or coppery tones, a bold assertiveness as the fresh fronds surge from the crowns, and a mature demeanor whose variations are vast.

It is true that all *Dryopteris* benefit from extra moisture while they establish themselves, and in dry shade they may never quite develop the almost tropical luxuriance they can achieve in more moist situations. But, along with the shield ferns (*Polystichum*), male ferns have both tolerance and beauty.

RECOMMENDED SELECTIONS

Dryopteris affinis Erect, dark green fronds with golden scales along the midrib, twice divided into alternate segments. 24 in. to 3 ft. (60 cm to 1 m) Z6

***Dryopteris affinis* 'Cristata'** Each erect dark frond is raggedly divided at the tips of the main divisions. Known as "the king of the male ferns" for over a hundred years. 3 ft. (1 m) Z6

***Dryopteris affinis* 'Polydactyla Mapplebeck'** Each segment of the fronds is tipped with neat, slender divisions. 3 ft. (1 m) Z6

Dryopteris filix-mas Perhaps the most robust species of all, erect mid-green fronds are twice divided into opposite pairs of leaflets. 2 to 3 ft. (60 cm to 1 m) Z4

***Dryopteris filix-mas* 'Cristata'** Each frond is crested both at the tip and at the tips of its divisions. 2 ft. (60 cm) Z4

***Dryopteris filix-mas* 'Grandiceps Wills'** Boldly and raggedly crested at the tips of the fronds, more delicately at the tips of the main divisions. 2 ft. (60 cm) Z4

Dryopteris marginalis The eastern wood fern is a hardier, neater, more delicate-looking North American native. Very drought-tolerant once established. 12 to 18 in. (30 to 45 cm) Z3

Euphorbia amygdaloides var. *robbiae*

MRS. ROBB'S SPURGE

Richly colored evergreen perennial with chartreuse flowers

Steadily spreading and self-supporting, Mrs. Robb's spurge has deep green, rather leathery 4 in. (10 cm) leaves that open paler green but soon darken. These leaves are carried in intriguing tight spirals towards the tops of the upright shoots. From midspring to early summer, the previous year's shoots are topped by chartreuse flowers in open heads, about 6 to 12 in. (15 to 30 cm) across. Cut out the flowering stems when the blooms have faded; although they would eventually die off, it makes the plant look tidier—but beware of the milky sap; it may irritate your skin or eyes. This perennial can spread strongly in rich, moist conditions; less so in dry shade.

Height 2 ft. (60 cm)
Hardiness Z6

THIS IS ONE of the absolutely indispensable dry shade perennials. The spiral arrangement of the rich dark green leaves ensures that they are perfectly placed to soak up every lumen of light available, while their leathery texture ensures that they lose minimal moisture through transpiration. At the same time, the rather moisture-retentive, steadily spreading roots (actually rhizomes) enable the plant to thrive in very difficult conditions. The result is an impressive perennial and also, as it spreads, an effective ground cover. Some writers suggest that forms of the Mediterranean *Euphorbia characias* and of *E. ×martini* are also

Mingling with boxwood, honesty, and *Iris foetidissima*, the chartreuse flower heads of *Euphorbia amygdaloides* var. *robbiae* stand brightly above the deep green foliage.

good dry shade plants but I find they become too spindly and sparse and tend to fall over.

It is said that this plant was first seen after it was brought back to England by a Mrs. Mary Anne Robb. In 1891, she made the then-hazardous journey to Istanbul to attend a wedding, spotted this plant, dug it up, and packed it in a hatbox for the return journey. To survive that, this must be a tough plant.

The deep richness of its leaf coloring makes it a perfect partner for lighter colored lamiums like yellow-flowered *Lamium galeobdolon* 'Hermann's Pride' or 'Silver Carpet' with their silvery leaf markings, and *L. maculatum* 'White Nancy' with broad silvery leaves and white flowers. Now, if only we had a variegated version...

Galium odoratum

Lacy, fresh, white, and (in dry shade) well-behaved

A low, steadily spreading perennial whose square stems tend to be erect at first but then become rather floppy. These stems carry clusters of up to nine short, elliptical, deep green leaves and 3 in. (7.5 cm) heads of small, starry, fragrant, pure white flowers from late spring into summer. The whole plant smells strongly of hay when dry.

Height 18 in. (45 cm)
Hardiness Z5

THIS IS A FINE example of a vigorous—sometimes rampant—plant tamed by its growing conditions. In a richer, more moist situation, and with more light, this lovely plant can be a real nuisance; drier and shadier conditions restrict its otherwise overenthusiastic spread. If it does make its way to richer, brighter conditions be prepared to take action!

Drier conditions help restrain *Galium odoratum*, which can be an uncomfortably vigorous perennial, without affecting the quality of its prettily divided foliage or its dainty white flowers.

Sweet woodruff is an endearingly bright, very pretty little plant, ideal at the front of a raised area where its lax growth can fall towards the next level. Its delicate appearance makes it an ideal companion to the broader, heavier looking foliage of hellebores.

Dry shade can be challenging, but will still allow for striking plant associations. Here, the bold foliage of *Helleborus* ×*hybridus* is surrounded by a miniature replica in *Galium odoratum*, which brings the added benefit of profuse starry blossoms.

Remarkably beautiful, truly resilient

Hellebores are a large group of clump-forming, mainly evergreen perennials, not all of which are suitable for dry shade. The bold, often leathery, usually dark green leaves are up to 20 in. (50 cm) across and divided, sometimes repeatedly, into leaflets joined at the end of the leaf stem. Hellebores bloom in winter or early spring in a vast range of colors and color patterns and with single, double, or anemone-centered flowers. Emerging from a slowly but steadily expanding rootstock, the striking bowl-shaped flowers are up to 2 to 3 in. (5 to 7.5 cm) across and may be nodding or face out sideways.

Height 15 to 30 in. (38 to 75 cm)
Hardiness Z5 to 7

HELLEBORES are among our best-loved perennials for their toughness, their adaptability, and their great variety of early flowers. Three in particular stand out as reliable in dry shade and fit into the cultural spectrum shared by many dry shade favorites: more sun demands more moisture, less sun demands less moisture. So the very fact that sunlight is restricted allows them to grow in drier conditions.

This hybrid between the Christmas rose and the Corsican hellebore, *Helleborus ×nigercors*, is a proven survivor in difficult conditions.

The delicate patterning of some *Helleborus* ×*hybridus* traces both the backs and insides of the flowers. Prepare their planting place well and they will bloom prolifically.

Naturally, in these shady situations, the otherwise captivating forms of Lenten rose (*Helleborus* ×*hybridus)*, with flowers in slate blue, deep purple, and deep red, make less impact than those in paler shades. Most effective are those in pure white, primrose yellow, and pale pink—with or without an even dusting of speckles or splashes. Of course, the patterns inside the downward-facing flowers can only be appreciated when the blooms are upturned for inspection. But thanks to the coloring on the backs of these nodding flowers, the whole plants still provide considerable impact from a distance. The newly fashionable *H.* ×*nigercors* is less hardy as it includes blood from the Corsican *H. argutifolius*, but its green flowers face outwards so they are more visible.

I usually recommend that the leaves of *H.* ×*hybridus* be removed in the fall to prevent the overwintering of fungal diseases but, in dry shade, plants must make the most of all available light so it pays to leave them in place through most of the winter to soak up the winter light—unless they are noticeably diseased.

H. foetidus, which has the rather unfortunate common name of stinking hellebore, may need discreet support if the shade is one-sided and the plant tries to lean towards the light, which can cause the stems to topple and fracture at the base. But with its fine foliage and attractive structure, the species is well worth trying. And don't worry, the stinking hellebore only smells if you rub the foliage. In a few forms the flowers actually have an attractive sweet fragrance.

RECOMMENDED SELECTIONS

Helleborus foetidus Less flamboyant than my other two choices, and with a different appearance thanks to generous clusters of small, red-tipped green flowers held at the top of leafy stems. 'Sopron' has pale green flowers that show up well. Yellow-leaved 'Gold Bullion' is a tempting but relatively weak plant unfortunately not suited to dry shade. 24 to 30in. (60 to 75 cm) Z5

Helleborus* ×*hybridus The familiar Lenten rose comes in an extraordinary range of colors and combinations. To be sure of a good form, buy from a specialist nursery or choose in flower. 18 in. (45 cm) Z4

Helleborus ×***nigercors*** Flattish, white-, green-, or cream-tinted flowers may age into peachy tones. Can be short-lived, an occasional soak with liquid fertilizer will help. 15 in. (38 cm) Z7

With dark green leaves and purplish stems and leafstalks, *Helleborus foetidus* Wester Flisk Group provides its own study in contrasts with clusters of light green flowers.

Yes, at least this one is tough enough

Thanks to its thick fibrous roots and spreading rhizomes, this semi-evergreen, remarkably tolerant perennial makes an impressive, widely spreading clump. In rich conditions it grows vigorously. The strong, branching stems emerge through attractive fans of narrow arching foliage, with striking V-shaped cross-sections. Atop the stems are clusters of large, orange, slightly messy, sterile double flowers about 6 in. (15 cm) across, reddish in the center, each with 15 to 18 petals. They open in a long succession over the summer. This is a triploid plant, a sterile cross between a genetically normal plant and one with twice the normal number of chromosomes.

Height 3 to 4 ft. (1 to 1.2 m)
Hardiness Z3

DAYLILIES are already America's favorite perennial, and now daylilies are also growing in favor in Britain as gardeners are seduced by their reliability and their extraordinary range of colors and color combinations. The changing climate helps Brits grow them more easily.

Although they tolerate of a wide range of soil types, daylilies generally need at least four hours a day of sunshine—but there are a few that are less demanding. In fact most daylilies will *grow* in dry shade, the issue is whether they will flower well and grow sufficiently to make anything other than sparse and unappealing clumps. Fortunately, there is one we can depend on. Described as "that thug" by one daylily authority, the double-flowered *Hemerocallis fulva* 'Flore Pleno' combines vigor and shade tolerance. And as an added bonus its large flowers and additional petals make this the best daylily to eat stir-fried.

Two others cultivars I can recommend are 'Chicago Apache', which is scarlet with a green throat, and the most popular daylily of all, the golden 'Stella D'Oro'.

Only a single daylily, *Hemerocallis fulva* 'Flore Pleno' has the vigor and the resilience to produce a long season of double orange flowers even in dry shade.

Fashionable and colorful—just choose carefully

Evergreen perennials with rather woody rootstocks from which develop mounds of long-stemmed, more or less heart-shaped or rounded foliage. The foliage may be waved, lobed, toothed, and often strikingly veined and the undersides of the leaves are often glossy and a redder shade than the upper surface. In some the leaves are noticeably glossy, in others slightly downy. In spring and summer, slender, upright stems emerge through the foliage and the upper parts carry small tubular flowers, sometimes without petals. Plants are self-sterile, so any seedlings that arise in the garden will be hybrids.

Height 18 to 30 in. (45 to 75 cm)
Hardiness Z3 to 7

O N BOTH SIDES of the Altantic, coral bells are on the way to becoming the most popular perennial of all and in recent years a huge number of new cultivars has been introduced. This new wave mainly features plants with colorful foliage that include shades and color combinations never before imagined. In some the flowers are so unremarkable, or even rather muddy in color, that they are best removed. In others, they are bright and long-lasting. These heucheras can be very impressive, but not all are vigorous and long-lived in all situations. Some of those that are suitable for dry shade have less startling foliage but better flowers.

Those which fit our purpose are mainly derived from three species that are inherently shade- and drought-tolerant in their natural habitats: *Heuchera maxima*, *H. pubescens*, and *H. villosa*. Some recent collections from the wild have focused on individual plants from unusually hostile situations in the hope that their adaptive tolerance will be passed to plants bred from them—this is certainly true in the case of 'Stainless Steel'.

Building up mulch around the plants not only tends to lock in whatever moisture the soil contains, but the heucheras will root into it, because they tend to grow out of the soil as they mature,

RECOMMENDED SELECTIONS

Heuchera **'Firefly'** Rounded, gently lobed, pale green leaves and bright red flowers. 2 ft. (60 cm) Z4

Heuchera **'Frosted Violet' ('Frosted Violet Dream' in Europe)** Makes a loose mound of purplish bronze foliage marked in silvery violet; long season of pink flowers. 20 in. (50 cm) Z4

Heuchera **'Old La Rochette'** Broad green leaves and tall, airy sprays of pink flowers. 2 ft. (60 cm) Z7

Heuchera 'Regina' is one of the most resilient of all heucheras and will make an attractive foliage display even in poor conditions.

Many heucheras are best en masse, but the beautifully patterned foliage of *Heuchera* 'Frosted Violet' is so neat and well-displayed that a single plant makes an attractive front-of-the-border specimen.

Heuchera **'Regina'** Rounded lobed leaves colored reddish purple and overlaid with silver; pink flowers. 32 in. (80 cm) Z4

Heuchera **'Santa Ana Cardinal'** Rounded green leaves mottled in a paler shade, with airy sprays of red flowers. Less hardy than many. 2 ft. (60 cm) Z7

Heuchera **'Stainless Steel'** Silver leaves sporting dark veins and purple undersides, with large white flowers on chocolate stems. 18 in. (45 cm) Z5

Heuchera **'Steel City'** Steely silver foliage, reddish purple below, and pink flowers. Its breeder, Charles Oliver of The Primrose Path, says: "It has proved a better survivor than any other heuchera we have grown." 30 in. (75 cm) Z5

Heuchera villosa **'Autumn Bride'** Large, soft, rounded but lobed green leaves and branched heads of white flowers surprisingly late, in early fall. 27 in. (70 cm) Z3

Heuchera villosa **'Bronze Wave'** An unusually large plant, with broad, slightly ruffled bronze leaves and pinkish white summer flowers. 27 in. (70 cm) Z3

Heuchera **'Wendy'** The same rounded green leaves mottled in a paler shade as 'Santa Ana Cardinal' but with pink flowers; also less hardy than many. 24 in. (60 cm) Z7

Other vigorous forms with drought- and shade-tolerant blood in their background include 'Raspberry Ice', 'Silver Lode', and 'Silver Scrolls'. Try too the old pink-flowered 'Chatterbox' which, like 'Firefly', is exceptionally robust.

×*Heucherella*

Heucherellas are hybrids between *Heuchera* and *Tiarella*. Crossing the two together combines the features of both parents to varying degree; their sterility ensures that they tend to flower prolifically although the flower quality is not always good. Many depend on moisture, but two hybrids with tough and hardy parents prove useful in dry shade: 'Burnished Bronze' makes a large plant with reddish bronze foliage and pink flowers; 'Quicksilver' is more compact, with bronze leaves overlaid with silver, and white flowers. Z4

Hosta

Favorite shade perennials that thrive in dry conditions

Hostas have a well-branched, fleshy, and rather coarse root system that supports woody crowns from which arise a mound of leaves. A few spread more widely by woody rhizomes. Each leaf is carried on its own stem—their length and shape vary enormously from long and slender to almost circular, and from 2 in. (5 cm) long by 1 in. (2.5 cm) wide to as much as 20 in. (50 cm) long by 16 in. (40 cm) wide. The entire mound of foliage may reach anything from 6 in. (15 cm) to 3 ft. (1 m) in height.

The leaves also vary in their color, featuring every shade of green: pure and gleaming white through cream shades, to yellows and deep gold; waxy blue coloring is also common. Many combine these foliage colors in an ever widening range of patterns and combinations. In texture, too, leaves range from smooth and almost glossy to densely puckered. In all forms, the leaf stems may stretch, changing the character of the plant.

Most hostas flower, usually in midsummer or late summer. The small lily-like flowers, in white, lilac, lavender or purple shades only last a day, like their relatives the daylilies, but may be fragrant.

Height 6 in. to 4 ft. (15 cm to 1.2 m)
Hardiness Z3

GARDENERS may be relieved, and perhaps slightly skeptical, to know that these familiar perennials can do well in dry shade. A little skepticism is wise, for only some hostas can thrive in these tough conditions and those that do benefit from help to get established. Improve the soil with organic matter before planting and, unless watered with a soaker hose, give the young plants plenty of water from the

The overlapping, blue-tinted foliage of *Hosta fortunei* var. *hyacinthina* makes a dense cover that not only catches the eye but also smothers weeds.

hose (never a sprinkler), particularly in the first and second spring and summer.

Green-leaved forms are most likely to succeed, followed by blue-leaved types. The more white, cream, yellow, or gold there is in the leaf, the less chlorophyll it contains and so the less vigorous the plants are likely to be—though there are some impressive exceptions. In some cases, forms that have survived in gardens from long before hostas became fashionable have proved their resilience. Dry shade also helps keep down the slugs that are notorious for munching on hosta leaves.

In general, choose vigorous, unvariegated cultivars and avoid very small, and very slow-growing types. It has been suggested that *Hosta tokudama* cultivars, which come into leaf late and grow slowly, are especially suitable as they need little water but only, I think, where there are no evergreens overhead to restrict the moisture supply as the hostas finally leaf out. Forms of *H. sieboldiana* develop unusually woody root systems that hold moisture and release it slowly to the plant.

Choose the right hostas, like this 'Albomarginata', and they will develop into such impressive clumps that you will forget they are growing in difficult conditions.

RECOMMENDED SELECTIONS

Heights refer to the foliage mound, not the flowers.

Hosta **'Albomarginata'** Oval leaf with a long curved tip and slightly variable white edge, the pale lavender flowers, in midsummer, are elegantly set on tightly gathered, upright stems. 2 ft. (60 cm)

Hosta fortunei **var. *hyacinthina*** Dark green, slightly waved leaves have a bluish spring tint and good gold fall color. 20 in. (50 cm)

Hosta **'Ground Master'** Makes a low widely spreading mound of elliptical leaves, dark green in the center, and a variable yellow and cream margin. 16 in. (40 cm)

Hosta **'Honeybells'** Large and vigorous plant with large, slightly shiny, mid-green, wavy-edged leaves and fragrant very pale lavender flowers in midsummer. 2 ft. (60 cm)

Hosta kikutii **var. *yakusimensis*** Makes a dense mound of narrowly elliptical, dark green, slightly rippled leaves with long curved tips; lavender flowers in late summer. 16 in. (40 cm)

Hosta lancifolia Vigorous plants that carry elliptical, mid-green, attractively overlapping leaves; generously produced late summer lavender flowers. 16 in. (40 cm)

Hosta **'Regal Splendor'** Develops into a large mound of oval bluish leaves with creamy margins. Developed from the unvariegated 'Krossa Regal', which is also good. 30 in. (75 cm)

Hosta sieboldiana **'Elegans'** Heavy, corrugated, blue-green leaves and clusters of almost white flowers. Develops extra "bloom" on its leaves, as if sprinkled with blue dust. 28 in. (70 cm)

Hosta tokudama Boldly corrugated, blue-green, slightly cupped leaves make a slow-growing mound; off-white flowers. 16 in. (40 cm)

Hosta undulata **forms** Resilient variegated forms with slightly twisted foliage and lavender flowers. 12 to 18 in. (30 to 45 cm)

An unfortunate name for a valuable perennial

An evergreen perennial with fans of rather leathery, dark green, sword-shaped leaves above a network of fat, fibrous roots. The plants slowly spread into tight clumps, the foliage eventually arches attractively. In early summer, upright stems carry heads of up to five small, usually quite dowdy flowers in brown and purplish tones. These are followed by fat green pods that weigh down the stems and split to reveal rows of orange-scarlet seeds that remain colorful for many months as the pods dry and turn brown. The foliage only smells—some say of roast beef—when broken or crushed.

Height 18 in. (45 cm)
Hardiness Z6

AN IRIS WITH dreary flowers and odd-smelling foliage may not immediately stand out as an essential dry shade plant. But, uniquely among irises, the fruits are the key ornamental feature. The fat pods burst to reveal orderly rows of ¼ in. (6 mm) scarlet berries that weigh down the stems. True, stinking iris is not flamboyant in flower (with one rare exception). But it does combine resilience in dry and shady conditions with a colorful feature seen in no other irises. And while the most common form may carry unremarkable flowers, there are forms with flowers in a brighter, purer shade as well as those with berries in other colors. Many suggest the small, spring-flowering *Iris cristata*, in lilac-blue, is a good shade plant for the front of the border; my experience is that it appreciates moisture.

But over and above the appeal of the less common forms is the fact that this unusual iris is a robust, tolerant, easy-to-grow, and easy-to-propagate species that belongs in most dry shade gardens.

RECOMMENDED SELECTIONS

Iris foetidissima **var.** *citrina* The flowers are brighter than the plain species, a blend of pale yellow and brown. 'Fructu Albo' is like the species, but with white berries.
Iris foetidissima **var.** *lutescens* Buttercup yellow flowers, by far the best for flower color.

'Variegata', with white-striped foliage, seems appealing but does not thrive in dry conditions, rarely flowers or fruits, and is thought to be a carrier of virus diseases.

The startling orange-red berries of the evergreen *Iris foetidissima* brighten many fall and winter gardens, and are more dramatic than the plant's bluish flowers.

Luzula

Unassuming, but quietly effective

Woodrushes are mostly evergreen perennials, with spreading rhizomes supporting clusters of long, flat, arching, dark green leaves that are usually dusted with short white hairs, especially along the edges. As the plants develop, the foliage and rhizomes make a dense, slightly disorganized, weed-suppressing cover. In spring or summer, leafy stems arise topped by open, arching clusters of green, brown, or sometimes almost white flowers.

Height 32 in. (80 cm)
Hardiness Z4 or 5

THE COMMON name suggests that these valuable relations of the rushes (*Juncus*) have cylindrical leaves, but the foliage of the woodrushes is flat. Fortunately, unlike the moisture-loving rushes, they will take drought. Not aggressive spreaders, woodrushes are nonetheless determined, gradually expanding into weed-smothering tussocks. A number of attractive foliage forms are especially worth growing although their flowers also have a quiet appeal.

Companions with contrasting foliage forms and textures are ideal: hostas, especially blue-leaved types, and ferns in particular. Woodrushes may lose their looks in fierce winters but spring back with fresh growth.

RECOMMENDED SELECTIONS

Luzula luzuloides Narrow, pale green leaves and off-white, red-tinted flowers in early summer. 32 in. (80 cm) Z4

Luzula sylvatica Robust plant, with broad, dark leaves tapering to a point, and pale chestnut flowers. 'Auslese' has broader, pale leaves that are daintily twisted at the tips. 32 in. (80 cm) Z4

Luzula sylvatica **'Hohe Tatra' ('Aurea')** Yellowish leaves in cool conditions, becoming greener in summer; a little less hardy than the others. Z5

Luzula sylvatica **'Marginata'** Leaves have a narrow white band along each edge; provides the best combination of robustness and color. Z4

The evergreen foliage of *Luzula sylvatica* 'Hohe Tatra' develops yellow tones in winter and spring, then darkens to a deeper green in summer.

A classy perennial version of a utilitarian shrubby ground cover

Long, questing rhizomes support short upright stems topped with what are almost rosettes of fresh green leaves. At its brightest in spring, the foliage darkens as the season progresses and becomes purplish in fall while retaining some pale mottling. Each leaf is more or less oval and coarsely toothed towards the tip. In spring, spikes of small, off-white flowers open on pinkish stems among or before the leaves with the male flowers at the top of the spike and the female flowers below.

Height 6 to 12 in. (15 to 30 cm)
Hardiness Z5

THE UBIQUITOUS evergreen shrub *Pachysandra terminalis* (known sometimes as the Japanese spurge) can be charitably described as a utilitarian ground cover. Well, *P. procumbens* is its more stylish herbaceous relative which—although not flamboyant—has three valuable features: it steadily develops into a dense weed-smothering cover, without running wildly; it has the intriguing habit of changing color from fresh green to almost purple as the season runs its course from spring to fall; and its short spring spikes of white flowers are attractive. There are a number of named forms, none easy to find, mostly selected for more striking leaf markings. In fact, any forms of this tough and trouble-free species are worth trying.

RECOMMENDED SELECTIONS
Look out for two rarely seen options from Georgia master plantsman Don Jacobs, prefixed Eco.

Pachysandra procumbens **'Eco Treasure'** Foliage more boldly marked in silver.

Pachysandra procumbens **'Eco Picture Leaf'** Young foliage noticeably well-marked in spring.

Pachysandra procumbens **'Forest Green'** Larger leaves in a darker color; sometimes, wrongly, thought to be the same as the species.

Pachysandra procumbens **'Kingsville'** More striking leaf markings.

Pachysandra procumbens is the American native relation of the ubiquitous, but invaluable, *P. terminalis* and deserves to be planted much more widely—especially in dry shade situations.

Polystichum

Tough, adaptable, elegant and evergreen—what more do you want?

Short, stout rhizomes support crowns from which arise shuttlecock-like clusters of fronds, each divided into opposite leaflets, these often again divided. The smallest leaflets are often rather similar to an evergreen holly in outline. The fronds mature into a range of green shades, some glossy and some soft in texture. Most are evergreen and some are unusually winter hardy, many down to zone 3. The new emerging spring growth often features an attractive overlay of reddish or silvery scales which fall away as the frond develops. In some the mature fronds feature a central midrib in contrasting rusty or reddish coloring.

Height 16 to 24 in. (40 to 60 cm)
Hardiness Z3 to 6

There are many many forms of *Polystichum setiferum*, the soft shield fern, but all grow well in dry shade and although they may look quite delicate, they are actually very robust.

L IKE *Dryopteris*, the male fern, shield ferns are among the most beautiful of hardy ferns as well as being among the easiest to grow. In some species, their elegant fronds can develop into impressive specimens, especially if you help them get established with additional water. The combination of a soft and delicate look with robust tolerance of less than ideal conditions is very endearing.

Although the familiar wild species can be very beautiful, this is a group of over 200 species in which a large number of crested and other attractive forms has arisen over the years. Some of the forms of *Polystichum setiferum*, for example, are so distinct that even if you choose only this species, your dry shade garden can boast plenty of variety.

RECOMMENDED SELECTIONS

Polystichum acrostichoides Narrow, dark, leathery, rather stiff and upright fronds—narrowing at the tip where the spores are carried—emerge in spring from a flat ring of the previous year's fronds. *P. munitum* is like a larger version. 2 ft. (60 cm) Z3

Polystichum aculeatum Attractively arching, narrow, leathery fronds develop into impressive single-crowned specimens. 16 to 24 in. (40 to 60 cm) Z4

Polystichum setiferum Almost all forms are worth growing. Very variable, with large soft or sometimes more leathery fronds on long stalks. 'Divisilobum Wollaston' has lacy, almost triangular fronds. 'Herrenhausen' has dark green, leathery triangular fronds. 'Pulcherrimum Bevis' has glossy fronds neatly and symmetrically divided, rather like braided hair. 16 to 24 in. (40 to 60 cm) Z5

Polystichum tsussimense A much smaller species with paler fronds split into slender segments, ideal at the front of the raised shade garden. 16 in. (40 cm) Z6

The Christmas fern, *Polystichum acrostichoides*, is a familiar sight in drier American forests and carries its adaptability to dry, shady situations into the garden.

Invaluable combination of flowers and foliage

Low, deciduous or evergreen perennials that spread slowly at the root, grown for their spring flowers and attractive foliage. The rough, slightly bristly, smooth-edged foliage varies from broadly oval to narrowly lance shaped, and the leaf blade may taper narrowly into the rather stringy stem or have a bold, heart-shaped base. In color, the leaves vary from fresh bright green to bluish green to dark green and in many forms is patterned in silver. This varies from a few silver spots to a far more dense spotting to an almost entire silvering. The purple, blue, white, red, or pink funnel-shaped spring flowers all open from pink buds and are carried on upright or sometimes sprawling stems, the stem leaves being much smaller and narrower versions of the basal leaves.

Height 10 to 15 in. (25 to 38 cm)
Hardiness Z2 to 5

IN THE SHADE, plants with bright reflective foliage are a special asset and pulmonarias are prime perennials for silver coloring. Some feature a delicate patterning of silver spots on their broad leaves, in some the leaf blade is entirely silvered. But the broad mound of overlapping foliage that develops after the delightful spring flowers is both an attractive feature and a functional weed suppressant.

Pulmonarias are like primroses—some plants have "pin" flowers, with the female part (the stigma) prominent in the flower, while others have "thrum" flowers with prominent male parts. This feature ensures cross-pollination in wild plants. In the garden, the result is that all self-sown seedlings are likely to be hybrids and so will not resemble their parents.

When grown in sunnier situations, powdery mildew has been a problem on some cultivars especially in dry seasons. Even planted in shade, mildew may still be troublesome. Fortunately, in recent years, forms have been selected that are much less troubled by mildew. However, it is likely that, as with mildew-resistant forms of other plants including *Monarda* and *Phlox*, the mildew may develop new variants which overcome the resistance. The choices below are selected for mildew resistance as well as good foliage, flowers, and growth in dry shade.

Although pulmonarias spread, their expansion is steady and remorseless rather than vigorous. The extent to which they are evergreen depends partly on the inherent tendencies of particular cultivars and partly on climate; in the coldest regions all are deciduous.

RECOMMENDED SELECTIONS

***Pulmonaria angustifolia* 'Blaues Meer'** Large, dark green, deciduous, unspotted leaves and prolific large bright blue flowers. 1 ft. (30 cm) Z2

The cool blue flowers of *Pulmonaria* 'Moonshine' are followed by broad, mildew-resistant foliage that holds its green-fringed silvery tones into fall.

Vivid blue flowers of *Pulmonaria* 'Cotton Cool' opening from pinkish red buds give a multi-colored effect above the narrow ghostly leaves.

Pulmonaria **'Apple Frost'** Partially evergreen, with heavily silver-mottled leaves and rose pink flowers. 10 to 12 in. (25 to 30 cm) Z4

Pulmonaria **'Cotton Cool'** Long, narrow, rather upright, partially evergreen leaves which are almost completely silver; blue flowers. 8 to 12 in. (20 to 30 cm) Z4

Pulmonaria longifolia subsp. *cevennensis* Very long, heavily silvered leaves and blue flowers. 1 ft. (30 cm) Z5

Pulmonaria **'Margery Fish'** Long, narrow, very densely blotched and spotted leaves and blue flowers. 1 ft. (30 cm) Z4

Pulmonaria **'Moonshine'** Silvery leaves with a narrow green margin and prolific, small, pale blue flowers. 12 to 15 in. (30 to 38 cm) Z4

Pulmonaria **'Stillingfleet Meg'** Very robust, with deep green leaves, only sparsely spotted; the flowers retain their pink coloring at first before turning blue. 1 ft. (30 cm) Z4

Pulmonaria **'Victorian Brooch'** Distinctive, almost circular leaves with large silver spots and an unusually long season of outward-facing magenta pink flowers. 1 ft. (30 cm) Z4

There are hundreds of different pulmonarias, in addition to those recommended these have all been cited as unusually resistant to powdery mildew: 'Bubble Gum', 'Cleeton Red', 'Dark Vader', 'Excalibur', 'High Contrast', 'Ice Ballet', 'Milky Way', and 'Silver Bouquet'.

Rohdea japonica

Quietly confident, indefatigable, glossy colonizer

Sacred lily is an evergreen clump-forming perennial that slowly spreads into attractive colonies by means of short, thick rhizomes just below the soil surface. These give rise to rather erect rosettes of dark green, fleshy, and often glossy, somewhat lance-shaped leaves 11 to 18 in. (28 to 45 cm) long. Each leaf has a keel on the lower surface and a noticeable network of veins on the upper face. The small heads of greenish white flowers, a little like miniature heads of sweet corn, are not showy and are almost hidden because they are carried at ground level. The red fall fruits, however, are much more colorful.

Height 10 to 18 in. (25 to 45 cm)
Hardiness Z7

N JAPAN, gardeners cherish hundreds of variegated forms of the sacred lily, but this plant has not gripped gardeners' imagination in the West. However, this is an admirable plant for dry shade, with variegations to suit any enthusiast for foliage plants, and even the plain green wild form has a quiet dignity and a bold effectiveness. It is true, of course,

Rohdea japonica may be slow to establish itself into a mature plant, but its narrow, glossy evergreen foliage makes a bold statement.

that some of the variegated forms are slow-growing and less suited to difficult locations. And, sadly, so few are available from our nurseries, so try any vigorous variegated forms you come across.

The heavy-duty, rich green, glossy foliage may be held upright or arching and makes a good companion to plants with more finely dissected leaves. In the coldest areas of its range the foliage of the sacred lily may be cut back in the winter like that of most other perennials. It will shoot again in spring when its upright leaves will once more make good partners for ferns.

RECOMMENDED SELECTIONS

Rohdea japonica The wild species, the most widely available and the most vigorous. 18 in. (45 cm)

Rohdea japonica **'Marginata'** Has a very slender white edge to the leaf. 10 to 12 in. (25 to 30 cm)

Rohdea japonica **'Talbot Manor'** Leaves are unpredictably streaked along their length in white and pale green. 10 in. (25 cm)

Valuable and variable, discreet and disingenuous

A semi-evergreen perennial, purple dog violet has a dense fibrous root system from which new tufts of leaves sometimes emerge. Each rosette of more or less rounded leaves, heart-shaped at the base, produces low side branches carrying smaller versions of the basal leaves and small violet-blue, unscented flowers. Once these flowers have been pollinated by bees or other insects, the plants also produce flowers without petals that never open, but which are self-pollinated. In Purpurea Group the leaves may be tinted with purple or strongly colored—the degree of tinting varies with different forms but is also most pronounced in good light. Starting with a well-colored form gives the best chance of your plants continuing to be well-colored.

Height 6 to 8 in. (15 to 20 cm)
Hardiness Z5

KNOWN FOR a long time as *Viola labradorica* 'Purpurea', this variable purple-leaved little plant now proves to be a form of the much more common and widespread dog violet, *V. riviniana*, which grows naturally over much of Europe and even into North Africa. *V. labradorica* is a relatively uncommon species from Greenland, Labrador, and Nova Scotia. Most other violas are insufficiently robust for

The smoky purple foliage of *Viola riviniana* Purpurea Group is peppered in spring with small blue flowers that readily spread around their seeds.

dry shade unless you make the area much less dry—in which case there are many options.

This is a tough and tolerant plant, making a less luxuriant and less richly colored display in dry shade but valuable nevertheless. Especially useful in wilder areas, the edges of each seed pod squeeze together to pop out the seeds and ants then play a part in moving them farther afield. Seedlings tend to pop up in cracks in the paving and in crevices in retaining walls. Thanks to the colorful spring flowers and then the unopening summer flowers tucked under the foliage, a great deal of seed can be produced leading to the appearance of a great many seedlings. This is either a boon or a bugbear—depending on your point of view. But it certainly pays to remove those plants with less purple in their coloring to concentrate the pigment in the next generation.

Deceptively tough little plants with a delicate look

Deciduous or evergreen perennials, with a strongly branched rhizome that carries tight or spreading clumps of foliage. This foliage is split into oval or lance-shaped leaflets in multiples of three. In some species, the new foliage is flushed or mottled in bronze or purple. In spring, the small flowers, which resemble four-legged spiders, emerge along wiry, leafless stems. They come in a wide range of colors including white, pinks, reds, purples, and yellow, with some pretty bicolored forms.

Height 12 to 20 in. (30 to 50 cm)
Hardiness Z5

EVERGREEN epimediums are invaluable dry shade ground covers. While many species are unsuitable for these trying conditions, the choices listed here are vigorous, they spread well, their foliage is attractive, and they should produce a great many flowers once the plants are settled and established. Like other dry shade favorites, some benefit at planting from additional organic matter in the soil and regular watering to ensure that the plants begin to spread well and flower profusely as soon as possible.

Some gardeners cut all the old foliage off both evergreen and deciduous species early in the season before the new growth emerges; others leave it in place to help protect the new shoots from frost and cold winds. But clipping over with a pair of hand shears allows the flowers to show themselves at their best, and also allows a little mulch to be worked in among the plants much more easily. This spring cleanup also stops the plants from looking ragged as they come into flower and the new foliage emerges. When the first florets have opened, snip off the stems low down for indoor display; the mature foliage is also useful in the vase.

It is mainly the species from Europe and their hybrids that grow well in dry shade. The many popular Asian species, *Epimedium grandiflorum*, *E. ×youngianum* forms, and others certainly enjoy the shade but not the drought.

RECOMMENDED SELECTIONS

Epimedium ×perralchicum Yellow flowers and wavy-edged, rounded evergreen leaflets. 'Fröhnleiten' is deep yellow and has copper-tinted young leaves. 'Wisley' is pale yellow. 14 to 16 in. (35 to 40 cm) Z5

Epimedium pinnatum* subsp. *colchicum Bright yellow flowers over evergreen, broad, oval leaflets. 12 to 16 in. (30 to 40 cm) Z5

PREVIOUS *Lamium maculatum* flowers cheerfully around a hosta and helps camouflage the fading foliage of daffodils that bloomed earlier in spring.

Epimedium pinnatum subsp. *colchicum* offers fresh green foliage with pretty rusty tints, cheerful yellow flowers, and exemplary weed smothering abilities.

Epimedium perralderianum Evergreen, with bright yellow flowers and copper-tinted young leaves. 1 ft. (30 cm) Z5

Epimedium* ×*versicolor Yellow, pink, or coppery flowers, may be deciduous or evergreen with up to nine oval leaflets, slightly reddish when young. 'Neosulphureum' is pale yellow, evergreen, and with coppery young leaves. 'Sulphureum' is pale yellow, evergreen, with coppery young leaves and is probably the toughest of the three *E.* ×*versicolor* cultivars. 'Versicolor' ('Discolor') has pink-and-yellow bicolored flowers and is deciduous with reddish young leaves. 1 ft. (30 cm) Z5

Epimedium* ×*warleyense Coppery orange and yellow flowers, evergreen with large oval leaflets. 16 to 20 in. (40 to 50 cm) Z5

***Epimedium* ×*warleyense* 'Orangekönigin'** Smaller, with fewer leaflets and pale orange flowers. Z5

Fragaria

Good coverage, pretty flowers—and sometimes tasty fruit

Ornamental strawberries spread by ground-hugging stems that emerge strongly from each crown. The stems root at each leaf joint and a new crown develops. The result is an increasingly dense and widespread mat of evergreen foliage (deciduous in colder climates), each leaf split into three rough-textured, toothed leaflets. In late spring, clusters of up to ten white or sometimes pink usually five-petaled flowers open, often resembling miniature wild roses. The flowers may be produced well into summer and are followed in many forms, but rarely in hybrids, by edible, fleshy red fruits.

Height 6 to 12 in. (15 to 30 cm)
Hardiness Z3 to 5

THIS SMALL group of reliable ground covers includes a surprising diversity of species and hybrids. They spread well, rooting into nutritious and water-retentive mulch. Some send out extraordinarily long runners across the soil surface. They may also flower well but the development of good fruits is often hindered by the lack of moisture. Beware the hybrids; if they reach lighter, more moist areas they will become a menace.

There are three wild species, two of which are fairly dainty (*Fragaria vesca* from Europe and *F. virginiana* from North America) along with the chunkier American *F. chiloensis*. *F. ×ananassa*, the cultivated strawberry, is a hybrid between

Hybrid strawberries like *Fragaria* 'Red Ruby' are so vigorous that you can even plant them in moister parts of the garden and then guide the spreading stems into drier areas.

The hybrids between *Fragaria* and *Potentilla* are perhaps not as surprising as you might think. For some time botanists have been contemplating uniting the two genera into one, concluding that they are not sufficiently distinct to be separated. The hybrids between the cultivated strawberry and *P. palustris* are the most vigorous of all. Mostly sterile, they feature prolific red or pink flowers but rarely fruit. At present, they are almost always still listed as *Fragaria*, and they are listed here as *F.* hybrids.

F. chiloensis and *F. virginiana* and in the culinary types, fruit development is likely to be restricted.

RECOMMENDED SELECTIONS

Fragaria ×*ananassa* The cream-splashed 'Variegata' is the best pick, unless you decide to gamble on fruit—or are prepared to water well. 6 in. (15 cm) Z4

Fragaria chiloensis Shiny, wrinkled foliage makes high ground cover but both male and female plants are needed to ensure fruit. 1 ft. (30 cm) Z4

***Fragaria* hybrids** These are very vigorous, low-growing plants with pink or red flowers and usually no fruits. Caution advised. 6 in. (15 cm)
    'Lipstick' is cherry pink, Z3
    'Pink Panda' is bright pink, Z4
    'Red Ruby' is deep rose-red, Z5

Fragaria vesca Vigorous, makes a dense low carpet studded like diamonds in spring with small white flowers; red berries later. 10 in. (25 cm) Z5

Fragaria virginiana Slightly bluish foliage and up to fifteen small white flowers; male and female flowers may be on separate plants. 10 in. (25 cm) Z3

Gaultheria shallon

A North American native with unexpected properties

Salal is a bushy, compact, evergreen shrub that suckers strongly to create wide clumps. The bristly reddish stems carry distinctive, broadly oval, dark green, leathery leaves up to 4 in. (10 cm) long and tapering suddenly to a point. In late spring and early summer, branched heads carry dainty strings of small, urn-shaped, bristly white flowers with maroon hairs across the top. These are followed in the fall by ½ in. (12 mm) juicy, flavorful, slightly hairy fruits (in fact fleshy sepals) that mature from pale reddish purple to dark blue or purple.

Height 3 ft. (1 m)
Hardiness Z6

Although native to moist Pacific Northwest forests, salal will tolerate drier conditions, especially when established. And although it sometimes reaches 6 ft. (2 m), it is more typically half this height. The combination of its suckering habit, which utilizes the moisture and nutrition of a slowly decaying woodland mulch, and its leathery

Even without its little white bells or its red berries, the leathery foliage of native salal (*Gaultheria shallon*) on its rusty red stems can be used in both native and non-native plantings.

leaves, which lose relatively little moisture, makes this a valuable albeit hardly flamboyant member of the dry shade community, especially on acid soil. True, with moisture in short supply the many-seeded fruits may not develop their full juiciness. But the berries are said to be an appetite suppressant, and are also made into jams and pies, sometimes combined with the more tart berries of *Mahonia aquifolium* with which salal often shares its habitat. The young leaves are also edible.

RECOMMENDED SELECTION
Look out for the rarely seen 'Snoqualmie Pass', which grows less tall yet spreads more widely.

Geranium

HARDY GERANIUM, CRANESBILL

Easy, long-flowering, and dependable—if you choose the right ones

Clump-forming perennials that produce good foliage from a rather woody root-stock. The mass of foliage makes an attractive spring mound before becoming more loose, but is still often dense enough to smother weeds. The leaves are dark or mid-green, and split into five or seven lobed divisions. From mid-spring to late spring onwards, sometimes for a very long season, the five-petaled flowers in purple, red, white, or one of a huge range of pink shades, sometimes with contrasting markings, are carried on relatively upright, sparsely leaved stems or on leafier trailing shoots.

Height 10 to 30 in. (25 to 75 cm)
Hardiness Z4 or 5

HARDY GERANIUMS are among the most easy to grow of all perennials and ground covers. They cover the ground well, provide a background of good foliage, offer sparkling flowers that keep coming for many months, and are easily rejuvenated by division and replanting. And while many appreciate more moisture than is available in

Of the many commendable forms of *Geranium* ×*oxonianum*, 'Beholder's Eye' stands out for its neat habit and its long season of vibrant pink flowers.

The best of all hardy geraniums for dry shade is *Geranium macrorrhizum*, here growing in a crevice in a shaded dry wall. In the fall, after the flowers fade, the foliage often develops reddish tints.

dry shade, there are still many lovely choices. Of course, as with so many dry shade options, a little extra care on first planting—soil improvement with organic matter plus a few good soaks—helps the plants become more resilient as they mature.

Some of the best known hardy geraniums are suited to dry shade but may also be some of the most dangerous. Do not underestimate the tendency of *Geranium endressii* and of *G. ×oxonianum* to self-sow and establish themselves into more favored parts of the garden. Choose them by all means, they will thrive, but there are also other choices less likely to stray.

It may be tempting to cut back some of these hardy geraniums hard after flowering to prevent overenthusiastic self-sowing, but in dry conditions their regrowth may stall. So be sure to give them plenty of water after cutting back.

RECOMMENDED SELECTIONS

Geranium ×cantabrigiense A hybrid with the invaluable *G. macrorrhizum*, with which it shares its aromatic foliage, but less vigorous. Large-flowered 'St Ola' is pure white. 1 ft. (30 cm) Z5

Geranium endressii Almost indestructible, the salmon or rosy flowers bloom all summer, but tend to fade as they age. May self-sow overenthusiastically. Choose only the best forms as some are less colorful: 'Betty Catchpole' is mauve-pink, 'Castle Drogo' is salmon. Try to buy forms of *G. endressii* from specialists because unremarkable, but vigorous, forms of *G. ×oxonianum* often masquerade under this name. 10 to 20 in. (25 to 50 cm) Z5

Geranium macrorrhizum Definitely the best pick for dry shade, making an aromatic mat of foliage, which may become reddish in fall, and with reddish, pink, or white flowers. 'Bevan's Variety' is magenta-pink, 'Ingwersen's Variety' is pale pink, and the pure white 'White-Ness' is especially effective. 12 to 15 in. (30 to 38 cm) Z4

Geranium nodosum Bright, glossy leaves and purple-veined lilac flowers all summer. Generally well-behaved. 8 to 18 in. (20 to 45 cm) Z4

Geranium* ×*oxonianum Magenta-pink to white flowers and every shade between, for a long season of bloom. Dry conditions thankfully curtail its vigor. Never choose an unnamed form as it may be an unremarkable seedling. A. T. Johnson' in pale silvery pink, 'Ankum's White' in pure white, 'Beholder's Eye' in deep pink, and 'Wargrave Pink' in salmon pink are among the best. 12 to 28 in. (30 to 70 cm) Z4

Geranium phaeum Makes a lovely spring foliage mound, followed by upright stems of purple, pinkish, lilac, or white flowers with backswept petals. 'Album', with white flowers and pale green leaves, and 'Lily Lovell', in violet with a white eye, are both good. Some forms are best avoided: the sultry dark forms will not show up well, the variegated and yellow-leaved forms are often weak. 12 to 30 in. (30 to 75 cm) Z4

Geranium versicolor Spreading growth and rather shiny foliage is topped by white flowers delightfully veined in purple. 18 in. (45 cm) Z5

Hedera

Invaluable evergreen ground cover not appreciated everywhere

Evergreen, self-clinging climbers that can be grown as highly effective ground cover. When grown as a climber, ivy's aerial roots ensure that the stems cling to trees or walls; when grown as a ground cover, these aerial roots grow into the soil. The extensive slender woody stems carry alternate more or less heart-shaped leaves, which may be neat and shapely or large, up to 1 ft. (30 cm) across, and less elegant; they vary from almost rounded to lobed in a wide variety of ways to rippled or jaggedly cut. In color the leaves may be dark to pale green, or variegated in shades from gold to silvery white in a variety of patterns. Flowers and fruits are not produced on plants grown as ground cover. Forms of *Hedera helix* tend to be neater, less vigorous, and more hardy than the larger leaved, vigorous *H. algeriensis* and *H. colchica*.

Height 6 in. to 2 ft. (15 to 60 cm)
Hardiness Z5 to 7

SOME PEOPLE simply condemn all ivy as invasive and feel that it should not be grown. This is a dramatic reaction to the fact that in some areas, some ivies are a problem. Especially in the American Northwest, ivy is considered a highly invasive plant both in and out of gardens.

As ground cover, ivies are superb plants, and in dry shade they are especially valuable. They will grow under evergreen shrubs, between evergreens and walls, in dark and dusty corners. In fact I would say ivies are the most valuable ground covers for dry shade. So what is the problem?

In the wild, ivy spreads in two ways: it creeps over the soil to steadily colonize new areas, but much more frequently it flowers and produces fruits that are spread by birds. Of course the fact that it spreads across the soil so effectively is part of its appeal as ground cover. But the roots are so shallow, at least at first, that it is easy to contain and indeed snipping it back encourages denser, more effective weed-smothering.

But ivy is an unusual plant in that, putting it simply, it only flowers and fruits when it grows up into the light. You never see ivy flowering half way up a wall, or flat on the ground. Typically it climbs a tree or wall and the growth only changes when it reaches the light, becoming more bushy and flowering. Many variegated ivies fail to flower at all and so never produce fruits.

In short, growing ivy as ground cover is the safest way to grow it. But to ensure these ground cover ivies stay in bounds, do not allow them to climb—either on walls or fences, or through shrubs. This is the beginning of their maturity into flowering plants.

RECOMMENDED SELECTIONS

Hedera algeriensis Less hardy, less successful as ground cover, and tending to make taller and less spreading

Hedera helix 'Glacier' is one the most valuable plants for dry shade, here as ground cover with *Epimedium* ×*perralchicum*.

growth; its 4 in. (10 cm) or larger leaves can smother other plants. The yellow-variegated 'Gloire de Marengo' is impressive given enough space. Z6

Hedera colchica Large-leaved, vigorous, and hardy, given space this is an effective ground cover. 'Dentata Variegata' and 'Sulphur Heart' bring us some of the finest forms for broad spaces. Z5

Hedera helix The hardiest, with a very wide range of leaf shapes and variegations, although some variegated forms may lose their brightness in shade. Z5, except as noted. 'Duck Foot' has tiny leaves and neat rounded lobes; for small yards. 'Glacier', with grey and white variegation is lovely, but less hardy (Z7). 'Golden Ingot' is edged and speckled in yellow and retains it color in shade. 'Manda's Crested' has wavy leaves that turn coppery in winter. 'Parsley Crested' has a crimped edge to the leaf. 'Ritterkreuz' has diamond-shaped lobes; use in small gardens where vigor is not required.

Hedera helix 'Golden Ingot' combines green, bluish, yellow, and cream tones in a single leaf.

It may well be *Hedera hibernica*, rather than the much more familiar *H. helix*, that is the dangerous invasive; ivy experts are coming around to this view. Generally more robust and more vigorous, it is a tetraploid (with twice the number of chromosomes of *H. helix*). Best avoided.

The prettily patterned leaves of *Hedera helix* 'Glacier' bring light traceries to dark walls. This cultivar rarely seems to revert to plain green as do other variegated ivies.

Lamium

Easy spreaders that bring silvery light to dark corners

Mainly evergreen perennials, with square stems that carry pairs of more or less triangular, toothed leaves each often splashed or speckled in silver. In many the leaves are brightened by a white or silver central flash, in some the silvering extends to almost the whole leaf surface without dramatically reducing the vigor of the plant. Clusters of purplish pink, pink, white, or yellow two-lipped flowers are carried at the tips of the shoots or in the upper leaf joints. The leafy stems root from the leaf joints as they touch the ground. You might be tempted to try 'Friday', the yellowish form of the weed *Lamium album* (white dead nettle). Resist—it's a thug.

Height 10 to 24 in. (25 to 60 cm)
Hardiness Z3 or 4

THE TWO DEAD nettles here are hardy, easy to grow, easy to propagate, and easy to remove if their vigor should become overenthusiastic. There are just the two useful species, but many good cultivars.

Yellow archangel, (*Lamium galeobdolon*), sometimes referred to as "the plant of desperation," is the more vigorous

With its tidy, toothed, and silvered foliage, followed by yellow flowers, *Lamium galeobdolon* 'Hermann's Pride' is a compact choice for small spaces.

of the two and much more likely to become a nuisance if it finds its way into richer conditions. It is also taller, especially the plain green-leaved form, which creates more of a mound or high cover. The highly silvered forms are patterned in ways similar to the unrelated brunneras and some are significantly less vigorous than the plain green-leaved version. All feature bright yellow flowers. *L. galeobdolon* has been known as *Lamiastrum galeobdolon* and also *Galeobdolon luteum*; it may still be found under these names.

Spotted dead nettle (*L. maculatum*) is better behaved. Developing a flat and spreading habit, even the unimproved species, which has white flashes through the center of its leaves, is valuable. Those with their leaves entirely silvered are especially effective and the vigor of the plants seems hardly reduced by the apparent lack of green leaf tissue, though some may be troubled by a leaf spot disease. Only those suffused in yellow or with yellow variegation seem less vigorous and less suitable for dry shade.

RECOMMENDED SELECTIONS

Lamium galeobdolon Vigorous and spreading by rooting stems, the foliage is green with, sometimes, a few small silvery specks. 20 in. (50 cm) Z4

Lamium galeobdolon '**Florentinum**' Has leaves marked with an attractive zone of silver speckles, rather like *Brunnera* 'Emerald Mist'. 2 ft. (60 cm) Z4

Lamium galeobdolon '**Hermann's Pride**' Has sharply toothed silver leaves with green veins, the plants often remain as clumps rather than spreading vigorously. 20 in. (50 cm) Z4

Lamium galeobdolon '**Silver Carpet**' Lower and more spreading with green-veined silver leaves developing purple tints in fall. 12 to 15 in. (30 to 38 cm) Z4

Lamium maculatum Flatter in growth, with a white streak rather than silver speckling. The most vigorous, those with the broadest leaves and those with white or pink flowers and/or silver leaves, are the most useful. 'Album' has pure white flowers, each leaf with a white central splash.

'Beacon Silver' has broad, silver leaves and purple flowers. 'Pink Nancy' has broad, silver leaves and salmon-pink flowers. 'Roseum' has rose-pink flowers, each leaf with a white central splash. 'White Nancy' has broad, silver leaves and white flowers. 10 in. (25 cm) Z4

'White Nancy' is a tough yet showy form of *Lamium maculatum* which, with its silver leaves and white spring flowers, easily roots into the soil to blend into surrounding plantings.

Adaptable and dependable, slow but relentless

Liriope are evergreen perennials in the lily family. They have fibrous roots (occasionally tubers) that support grasslike foliage that is upright at first then arches attractively. Some make tight clumps, others spread more widely. In the fall, upright spikes of small, bell-shaped flowers—usually deep blue or deep purple in color—emerge through the leaves on short spikes resembling those of grape hyacinths and are followed by dark, purplish black berries. There is some confusion over the names of lily turf. *Liriope* is often wrongly listed as the related *Ophiopogon*, and the names of some forms have become muddled. 'Silvery Sunproof', for instance, has become attached to many different variegated plants.

Height 8 to 24 in. (20 to 60 cm)
Hardiness Z6 or 7

WIDELY SOLD as a dependable ground cover, cultivars differ in the extent to which they spread or form clumps. Both types are valuable, although in dry shade the more spreading types may become rather sparse. However, dense planting of the clumping types can often provide an appealing cover and individual specimens are also effective. Another valuable feature of liriopes is their ease of propagation. Dig up a clump and pull it to pieces and it will yield a large number of small sprigs—individual pieces each with roots and a few leaves. These can be replanted and will soon develop into larger plants. Variegated forms, however, are often too slow and less well-colored when grown in the most difficult conditions and are best avoided.

RECOMMENDED SELECTIONS

Liriope exiliflora Slowly but determinedly spreading and with rather open spikes of mauve flowers. 12 to 16 in. (30 to 40 cm) Z7

***Liriope muscari* (*L. platyphylla*)** The most widely grown form, with dense spikes of purple flowers on tight clumps. 'Monroe White' has larger than average, pure white flowers. 'Peedee Ingot' has chartreuse foliage. 'Royal Purple' has deep purple flowers. 'Samantha' has pink flowers and is uncommon but worth seeking out. 18 to 24 in. (45 to 60 cm) Z6

Liriope spicata Spreads quickly, with short summer spikes of purple to white flowers. 'Gin-ryu' has slim white edges to the leaves. 8 to 12 in. (20 to 30 cm) Z6

The tough grasslike foliage of *Liriope spicata*, paired here with an epimedium, is supplemented in summer by blue or white upright flower clusters. It makes a fine edging along a pathway.

Held on violet stems, the blue flower spikes of *Liriope muscari* push through the leaves of an azalea in fall. The blooms may last into the winter months.

Ophiopogon

Dependable ground cover in an increasing range of attractive forms

Narrow-leaved, mainly Asian, evergreen perennials widely grown as ground cover. Mondo grass has long, often slender, grasslike foliage in green, variegated, or black that form clumps. Plants spread steadily but with determination. In summer, upright spikes of small, flared, six-petaled flowers in a wide range of mauve or purplish shades emerge through the leaves and are followed by blue berries. In colder areas, on the edge of their hardiness tolerance, ophiopogons may lose their foliage in winter then shoot again in spring. Liriopes are often listed as *Ophiopogon*, but are distinguished by their erect flowers; the flowers of *Ophiopogon* are nodding. Both are valuable dry shade plants.

Height 3 to 24 in. (7.5 to 60 cm)
Hardiness Z6 or 7

WITH JAPANESE breeders developing new forms, and new types being discovered in the wild, the rise of ophiopogons from dull but dependable to colorful and interesting has not been at the expense of their reliability. True, as is often the case, the variegated forms may be less successful in dry shade. But the increasing variety in foliage shape and plant habit is itself interesting. Some make low and congested tight ground cover, some are more open and more elegant and remain in tighter clumps. All are easily propagated by simply pulling the plants apart into sprigs and replanting them.

Lack of moisture can be difficult for ophiopogons and some gardeners grow the more striking ones in good soil in containers and soak them occasionally. Try variegated forms, especially in containers, but green-leaved cultivars tend to be more successful. The most popular ophiopogon by far is the black-leaved *O. planiscapus* 'Nigrescens' but black is not the ideal color for the shade garden where it simply adds to the gloom.

RECOMMENDED SELECTIONS

Ophiopogon jaburan Bold clumps of dark, arching leaves; lilac-tinted white flowers and blue berries. 16 to 24 in. (40 to 60 cm) Z7

Ophiopogon japonicus Like a smaller form of *O. jaburan* but with a steadily spreading habit and also much more variable. 8 to 12 in. (20 to 30 cm) Z7

Ophiopogon japonicus **'Gyoku-Ryu'** Steadily makes a lawn-like carpet of very dark leaves. 3 in. (7.5 cm) Z7

Ophiopogon japonicus **'Minor'** Has very dark green foliage and is very dwarf. 4 in. (10 cm) Z7

Ophiopogon planiscapus **'Haku ryu Ko'** **('Little Tabby')** Leaves striped in green and white, very slow growing (perhaps too slow). 6 in. (15 cm) Z6

The nodding pale lilac flowers of *Ophiopogon japonicus* tend to be hidden by the foliage, which spreads into a dense ground cover.

Seen everywhere—and for good reason

Sometimes described as a shrub, sometimes as an evergreen perennial, this is a low, semi-woody plant with stems which lay flat on the ground. The stems root and then turn upwards topped with clusters of dark green, glossy leaves that are reverse egg-shaped (narrow end towards the stem) and bluntly toothed towards the tip. The leaves remain on the plant for two or three years and so create a very dense carpet. In early summer, short spikes of small white flowers tinted with purple towards the tips are produced in the tops of the shoots.

Height 6 to 12 in. (15 to 30 cm)
Hardiness Z4

MANY PEOPLE, myself included, have remarked that this is a dull plant. And in more welcoming garden situations it does indeed suffer by comparison with other shade-loving ground covers. However, where moisture is in short supply, we must turn to the dependable and inexpensive Japanese pachysandra. Described in one classic book on shrubs as "of only moderate decorative value," in fact the combination of steadfast but not invasive spread, dense weed-smothering growth, resilience in difficult conditions, and low evergreen foliage that makes a good backdrop to other plants ensures that Japanese pachysandra is valued, if not for its own beauty then for its verdant functionality. The familiar species is by far the most widely seen but there are three other forms worth looking out for. Choose these and at least you can boast of growing the classiest ones.

RECOMMENDED SELECTIONS

Pachysandra terminalis **'Green Carpet'** Shorter and neater in growth, the leaves more finely toothed. 6 in. (15 cm)

Pachysandra terminalis **'Green Sheen'** Shorter and with glossy foliage which looks better in shade. Also more tolerant of hot and humid summers. Sometimes sold as the straight species. 8 in. (20 cm)

Pachysandra terminalis **'Variegata'** (**'Silver Edge'**) White edges to the leaves and slower in growth; may be too slow for dry shade. 10 in. (25 cm)

The variegated form of *Pachysandra terminalis* spreads more slowly than the solid green form, but it is a slightly more stylish version of this dependable evergreen ground cover.

Like a big, chunky, perennial forget-me-not

Stout roots support a belligerent rosette of large, dark green, oval leaves narrowing to a point at the tip and to a long stalk at the base. More or less upright, branched leafy stems carry smaller versions of the basal leaves and, in the leaf joints, long-stemmed clusters of up to 15 flowers unfurl like those of forget-me-nots to display small azure flowers. Stems and leaves are uniformly rough and bristly.

Height 28 in. to 3 ft. (70 cm to 90 cm)
Hardiness Z6

THIS IS A bruiser of plant in lush situations but better behaved in drier locations, making it a tall and tolerant ground cover. Having spread from its native habitats in southwest Europe, green alkanet was seen in the wild in Britain as long ago as 1724 and is now established over almost every part of England and much of Wales and Scotland, as well as the American west coast, though it is rarely a nuisance. Its large, rough leaves are certainly effective in smothering weeds, its bright blue flowers are undeniably pretty. Although there has been only one named form, white, bicolored, and variegated forms occasionally appear in the wild—they would be well worth bringing into the garden. I once found the pretty pale blue form, known as 'Morley China Blue', which was available for a year or two but now seems to have disappeared from nurseries.

This is, however, a plant which can spread rapidly by seed. And, if left to self-sow, it will probably hop from dry shade to happier situations where it will develop more quickly and into larger plants. Then, when you dig it up, small pieces of root will regrow. So this is an attractive and useful plant—but not perfect.

Like a pugnacious version of the more familiar *Brunnera macrophylla*, *Pentaglottis sempervirens* spreads steadily to create an effective ground cover dotted with bright blue flowers.

Rubus

Vigorous and bristly evergreen ground cover

The brambles discussed here are vigorous, prostrate, evergreen shrubs with arching or ground-hugging, fairly bristly shoots that root where they touch the soil to create a near-impenetrable mass of growth. They carry rounded or heart-shaped, usually well-lobed, glossy dark green leaves that are noticeably veined, often covered in grey felt on the undersides and may be wavy along their edges. They can develop bronzed tints in winter. In summer, flat white flowers are produced, singly or in clusters, and later these are often followed by red or orange edible fruits like small raspberries.

Height 12 to 24 in. (30 to 60 cm)
Hardiness Z7

WITH FOUR attractive features on one plant, brambles are perhaps less popular than they should be thanks to their sometimes uncomfortable tendency to spread overenthusiastically. True, these creeping brambles can be vigorous. But in dry shade their determination is somewhat sapped by the conditions and the plants are better behaved. And it is a simple matter to detach rooted pieces to plant elsewhere.

Not only do they feature handsome evergreen leaves, but the foliage is carried on red stems, there are white flowers in summer, and then red raspberry-like fruits in the fall. And with their low, root-as-they-go habit they colonize under dark trees very effectively. There are many many forms of *Rubus*—including the edible raspberries and blackberries—but the evergreen creepers listed here are the picks for dry shade.

RECOMMENDED SELECTIONS

Rubus **'Betty Ashburner'** A hybrid between *R. rolfei* and *R. tricolor*. Arching shoots and glossy leaves although the flowers and fruits are produced sparsely. Less vigorous than *R. tricolor*. 12 in. (30 cm) Z7

Rubus rolfei Much harder to find than the other two choices and has flat creeping growth and leaves clearly networked in veins. It may be listed as *R. calycinoides* or *R. pentalobus*. 12 in. (30 cm) Z7

Rubus tricolor Long creeping shoots with glossy leaves, eventually makes relatively high cover; the fruits are unusually large. 2 ft. (60 cm) Z7

Rubus rolfei is a tough bramble that provides effective coverage to a height of 12 in. (30 cm) in all shady conditions.

Cheerful and determined low spreader

Rough, rather unrefined, but often attractive perennials, with strong growing rhizomes that support a basal rosette of coarse, hairy, oval, or elliptical foliage from 6 to 18 in. (15 to 45 cm) long. Upright stems carry alternate, smaller versions of the basal leaves and, at the tips and in the upper leaf joints, arching clusters of tubular or narrowly bell-shaped flowers in blue, pink, cream, and white with some bicolors. The foliage of the larger types is superb organic enrichment for vegetable gardens and can also be used to make a liquid feed.

Height 6 to 18 in (15 to 45 cm)
Hardiness Z3 to 5

This easy-to-grow variegated comfrey, *Symphytum* 'Goldsmith', carpets the ground with creamy yellow edged green leaves.

RANGING from the unstoppable to the unkillable to the merely single-minded, comfreys are fine ground covers but may be something of a gamble. In wilder situations, where their aggressive habits will not cause confrontation with milder-mannered residents, most can be planted and left alone. They include low spreaders with small leaves and larger but compact plants with eruptions of bold arching foliage. The shorter, more restrained types are preferred for dry shade.

The variegated comfreys are instantly appealing for their bright coloration but all may revert to plain green and then double in vigor. If this happens with the bold, deep-rooted forms of *Symphytum* ×*uplandicum* then years of anguish follow as you struggle to eliminate your new monster, which continues to shoot up from fragments of those deep roots. At least with the much smaller 'Goldsmith' even the reverted form is worth growing and not too overwhelming.

RECOMMENDED SELECTIONS

Three lower, creeping types stand out.

Symphytum **'Goldsmith'** Bright, yellow-edged foliage and blue-and-white bicolored flowers; shallow-rooted and so less difficult to control than others. 6 to 12 in. (15 to 30 cm) Z5

Symphytum ibericum Also relatively shallow-rooted, with plain green leaves and pale creamy yellow flowers. 'Wisley Blue' has white flowers, blue at the base. 12 to 16 in. (30 to 40 cm) Z3

Symphytum **'Rubrum'** Dark green leaves and deep crimson flowers; is less vigorous than most. 18 in. (45 cm) Z4

Ready for a gamble? Go for the taller, more vigorous (and sometimes floppy) 'Hidcote Blue' and 'Hidcote Pink' and the better behaved, more clumping, and very attractive pure white *Symphytum orientale*.

The steadily spreading fresh green foliage of *Symphytum ibericum* 'Wisley Blue' is topped by the red, white, and blue of buds and flowers.

Trachystemon orientalis ABRAHAM-ISAAC-JACOB

Robust and determined spring spreader

Spreading, intercrossing rhizomes—which can be up to 2 in. (5 cm) thick—support large, long-stalked, more or less heart-shaped, often dark and even slightly bluish green leaves that are noticeably rough and rasping to the touch, much like brunnera leaves. In spring, before the leaves develop, clusters of starry purplish blue flowers, rather like those of borage, develop on extending stems with up to 15 in a cluster. Opening from purple buds, the blue petals roll back prettily to expose the purple-tipped white stamens. After flowering, the foliage expands to create a dense weed-smothering cover.

Height 8 to 24 in. (20 to 60 cm)
Hardiness Z6

THE BORAGE family includes many fine dry shade plants including *Brunnera*, *Pentaglottis*, *Pulmonaria*, and *Symphytum*, but *Trachystemon orientalis* is often discounted, perhaps because in rich, moist conditions it can be an aggressive spreader. But with its starry purple-and-white spring flowers followed by dense weed-smothering foliage, it also features an extensive root system making this a fine plant for retaining soil on dry banks. And it is tolerant of a wide range of conditions—objecting only to heat combined with drought.

In dry shade its less admirable habits are constrained by lack of light and moisture; it might almost be called well behaved. But it pays to watch its tendency to spread into more agreeable conditions where it may well overdominate. For the cautious, this is a plant best used in drifts of ground cover in areas bounded by paths, walls, or fences, or forceful shrubs that can hold their own. This may sound alarming, but in the right place this is a very valuable plant. In the wrong place it is a menace. In its native Turkey, the rhizomes, the stems, the young leaves, and the flowers are all eaten.

So far, there are no cultivars of this species—only the original wild form is available.

While the foliage of *Trachystemon orientalis* forms a dense, weed-smothering mat, the starry spring flowers are held on upright deep purple, almost black, stems.

Vinca

Attractive, tolerant, and adaptable—but invasive in some areas

There are two main species, one bigger and with larger leaves than the other. Both are more or less prostrate plants, sometimes classified as shrubs and sometimes as perennials. From a semi-woody base, trailing or arching shoots arise, each lined with pairs of elliptical or oval evergreen leaves; in many forms they are attractively variegated. The stems root where they touch the ground and soon develop into a smothering tangle of rooted growth. In spring and sometimes extending through to fall, rounded or star-shaped, five-petaled flowers emerge from the leaf joints of early shoots and sometimes on older growth. Most are blue, some are white or purple shades, and there are few with double flowers.

Height 6 to 18 in. (15 to 45 cm)
Hardiness Z4 or 7

VINCAS ARE among the most effective of ground cover plants for shade, and can do well in the dry and shady conditions that defeat so many other plants. This is especially true if the area is well mulched, as the vincas will root into the mulch and benefit from its moisture and nutrients. In general, vincas are sufficiently vigorous that the bright, variegated forms can be chosen as well as green-leaved types, which is a benefit as many of the unvariegated forms have very dark foliage. However, variegated forms have a tendency to revert to green, which hastens their spread into lusher situations—and perhaps out of the garden and into the woods. For instance, 'Illumination', with a brilliant yellow splash in the center of each dark leaf, is best avoided as it regularly reverts to plain *Vinca minor*.

In some areas *V. minor* in particular has become invasive although it seems especially troublesome when deer have greatly reduced the natural vegetation. The greater periwinkle, *V. major*, is much less of a problem but can still be invasive in some areas. It often spreads from old homesteads or ruined farms and from plants discarded by the side of the road. However, as both periwinkles seem to spread only rarely by seed, gardeners can easily restrict their spread by ensuring they don't creep through fences and by not thoughtlessly discarding surplus plant material by roadsides. It is a simple matter to remove straying strands if they threaten to leave your garden. And the necessity to watch for overenthusiastic spread is more than balanced by its value as dry shade ground cover and by its attractiveness in both flowers and foliage. Still, it pays to check with a local expert source to verify if the plant is considered a pest in your region.

RECOMMENDED SELECTIONS

Vinca major The larger-leaved species, but much less hardy,

Once known as 'Bowles's Variety', 'La Grave' is a popular lavender blue form of *Vinca minor* with an abundance of large spring flowers.

less tolerant, and it has fewer interesting cultivars than *V. minor*. It features large, dark, glossy leaves on arching stems and purple-blue flowers. 'Alba' is white-flowered but can be difficult to find. 'Maculata' has leaves with a yellowish green central splash. 'Variegata' has irregular creamy margins to the leaves. 'Wojo's Gem' has a bold cream, almost white, flash in the center of each leaf. 15 to 18 in. (38 to 45 cm) Z7

Vinca minor Smaller, hardier, and more adaptable with creeping stems, smaller, very dark green leaves, and single or double flowers in blue shades, purple shades and white. 'Alba' has white flowers. 'Alba Variegata' has white flowers and leaves edged in pale yellow. 'Argenteovariegata' has leaves with creamy, almost white edges and some leaves entirely cream. 'Atropurpurea' has flowers in dark plum-purple. 'Azurea Flore Pleno' has double, pale blue flowers. 'Gertrude Jekyll' is neater and less vigorous in growth and has prolific white flowers. 'La Grave' has large lavender-blue flowers. 6 to 8 in. (15 to 20 cm) Z4

Waldsteinia

Vigorous ground covers with two ways of spreading

Strawberry-like, semi-evergreen perennial, spreading vigorously both by rooting stems on the soil surface and by rhizomes below. The toothed or lobed, rather shiny, dark green leaves are divided into three angular leaflets, and the whole plant spreads to create a dense low cover which may be tinted with purple tones in winter. In late spring and early summer, bright yellow, five-petaled, saucer-shaped flowers beam up from just above the foliage. These are followed by small, dry fruit.

Height 4 to 8 in. (10 to 20 cm)
Hardiness Z3

THESE VIGOROUS, low ground covers, spreading both above and below the ground, may look like strawberries but taste nothing like them. However, *Waldsteinia* make up for their lack of tasty fruits by developing a more effective cover in a wider range of situations. And make no mistake, these plants can move. In dry shade, of course, their vigor is restrained by the conditions which is no bad thing, so if you have improved conditions in your dry shade garden so that they more resemble those of moister shade gardens, think twice before planting what will prove a vigorous spreader. The most widely grown species is from Europe as well as Siberia and Japan, while there is also a lesser-known but similar North American species.

The strawberry relative *Waldsteinia ternata* entwines with *Vinca minor* 'Argenteovariegata' to create a dense ground cover of foliage.

RECOMMENDED SELECTIONS

Waldsteinia fragarioides From North America, with larger leaves than its European relative. 4 to 8 in. (10 to 20 cm) Z3

Waldsteinia ternata From Europe, with smaller leaves but the same bright buttercup yellow flowers. 4 to 6 in. (10 to 15 cm) Z3

The toughest and most adaptable of the "little blue bulbs"

Dwarf bulb related to *Scilla*, each bulb produces two or three, usually dark green leaves up to about 6 in. (15 cm) long that become wider towards the tip. The single flowering stems carry, in some forms, as many as 20 flowers. Each star-shaped flower is up to 1½ in. (3.7 cm) across, almost always blue with a white center, and the blooms open in succession during early spring.

Height 6 in. (15 cm)
Hardiness Z3

PREVIOUS Clumps of daffodils interplanted with chionodoxas enjoy the spring sunshine before the overhead canopy of foliage closes in.

FAMILIAR starry blue and white flowered bulbs, self-seeding and spreading when happy but never becoming a nuisance. Plant in clumps, in pockets of good soil, and apart from an occasional spring soak and feed, and a regular annual mulch, chionodoxas need little care. Their seedlings will pop up and create surprising combinations with other plants.

Unfortunately there has been continuing confusion over the correct name for the most dependable and the most widely grown of chionodoxas. The plant generally seen as *Chionodoxa luciliae* has also been known recently as both *C. forbesii* and *C. siehei*—which are in fact distinct species. The fact that different forms of all of them have been available only adds to the confusion. If you buy *C. luciliae* from a non-specialist supplier you will almost always get the right plant!

RECOMMENDED SELECTIONS

Chionodoxa luciliae Up to 12 flowers, each with a white center and blue tips to the petals.

C. forbesii and ***C. siehei*** Names to keep an eye out for; both are good.

There may be confusion about the correct name for some *Chionodoxa*, but the bulbs you find under that name are colorful and easy to grow.

Cyclamen

The most engaging of flowers in spring and fall

Small perennials with steadily expanding, rather flat tubers. The shoots emerge from the concave top of the tuber and a scattering of fine wiry roots emerges from the convex base. The leaves are rounded, to heart- or arrowhead-shaped, sometimes lobed or toothed, and are often flushed or patterned in silver. The nodding flowers in a wide range of white, carmine, and pink shades are carried singly on vertical stems, each bloom with five backswept petals. After blooming, the flower stalks curl to bring the seed capsule down to soil level, the fresh seeds having a sugary coating that is attractive to ants.

Height 2 to 5 in. (5 to 12.5 cm)
Hardiness Z4 to 7

THERE ARE two species of *Cyclamen* that light up dry and shady sites with both their foliage and their flowers. They vary greatly in the color of both features but here is a useful rule: for dry shade choose those with pale flowers and those with well-silvered leaves. Flowers in pinks, bicolors, and white are available in both species and they also come in forms with entirely silver foliage—ideal in a

The prettily patterned foliage of *Cyclamen hederifolium* comes in wide range of shapes and of silver and green color combinations.

172 CHOOSING PLANTS FOR DRY SHADE

'Tilebarn Elizabeth', a lovely form of *Cyclamen coum*, nestles
snugly at the edge of a woodland garden.

With two or more different forms of *Cyclamen coum* in the garden, a range of delightful flower colors and foliage patterns will soon start to appear.

situation where a bright reflective surface helps lighten the darkness. A few forms are fragrant. Look for cyclamen from specialist mail-order nurseries, they will have the best range.

Unlike most of the plants in this book, cyclamen can only be propagated from seed. Well, you could slice a tuber in half and dust the cut surfaces with fungicide—the pieces may survive, they may not. But seeds are usually generously produced and, as with *Corydalis* and hellebores, ants can leave them in some unlikely places.

Their fat, flattish, slowly expanding tubers have developed to ensure the plants survive in difficult conditions. In the wild, *C. coum* is found under conifers and rhododendrons and often among the roots of trees and on rock ledges. *C. hederifolium* is often found in the *maquis* of southern Europe, similar to the American chaparral, under evergreen shrubs. Sounds like dry shade to me.

RECOMMENDED SELECTIONS

Cyclamen coum Rounded leaves from spring to fall and flowers in carmine, pinks, and white in winter and spring. 2 to 4 in. (5 to 10 cm) Z4

Cyclamen hederifolium More or less triangular leaves from fall to late spring and flowers in pinks and white in fall. There is one plant of *C. hederifolium* confirmed as over 130 years old. 4 to 5 in. (10 to 12.5 cm) Z6

Cyclamen repandum Some, but not all, gardeners find this fragrant, spring-flowering species does well in dry shade. 4 to 6 in. (10 to 15 cm) Z7

Classic first bulbs of each new season

Dwarf bulbs that flower in winter and spring, each bulb producing usually two slender grayish or green, more or less strap-shaped leaves. The nodding flowers on individual stems are white and pear-shaped, with three longer outer petals, which flare on warm sunny days, and three shorter inner petals usually marked in green. Some types are scented.

Height 4 to 8 in. (10 to 20 cm)
Hardiness Z3 or 4

EVERYONE loves snowdrops, and although their pristine flowers are at their most prolific and vigorous in more accommodating conditions, a little preparation before planting will transform the dry shade fortunes of this essential little bulb.

All that you must do is make a good-sized hole, larger than you would expect for the number of bulbs to be planted, fill

Thorough soil preparation before planting helps snowdrops (*Galanthus nivalis*) quickly develop into attractive clumps that steadily increase year after year.

it with improved soil and then plant. A clump of three, five, seven, or more bulbs, each set 2 to 3 in. (5 to 7.5 cm) apart, will give them the opportunity to spread through the good soil over the years. The conventional wisdom is to plant and transplant snowdrops "in the green," i.e., when the plants are in growth. But they can also be moved in summer when completely dormant as long as the bulbs never dry out.

There are literally hundreds of different snowdrops, but those listed here are more resilient than most. Just be sure you choose vigorous cultivars. Some may tempt you—in particular those with yellow instead of green markings, but they are often infuriatingly slow. Over $300 has been paid by enthusiasts for a single snowdrop bulb. Do not waste your money; spend it on improving the conditions!

RECOMMENDED SELECTIONS

Galanthus **'Atkinsii'** Very early, with long, slender, scented single flowers, each of the inner petals with a heart-shaped green mark at the tip. 8 in. (20 cm) Z3

Galanthus **'Dionysus'** I find this the most vigorous of the classier doubles, the interior as regular as a rosebud sliced in half. 6 in. (15 cm) Z4

Galanthus elwesii **'Zwanenburg'** Large flowers, two well-balanced green marks on the inner petals; may produce two flowers per bulb. 8 in. (20 cm) Z3

Galanthus nivalis A dainty little bulb that slowly forms large clumps, with slim grey-striped leaves and small flowers each with an inverted green V at the base of the inner petals. 'Flore Pleno' is a rather messy double. 4 in. (10 cm) Z3

Galanthus nivalis **'S. Arnott'** Large, early, prolific, and well-scented, the rounded flowers have an inverted green V at the base of the inner petals. 6 to 8 in. (15 to 20 cm) Z4

Narcissus

Widely grown, for all the right reasons

These familiar bulbs carry long, strap-like, often slightly grayish green leaves that emerge in spring with the flowers and then die down in summer. Each cylindrical flowering stem carries from one to fifteen, or even more, distinctive flowers, each with six often overlapping petals forming a more or less flat disc surrounding a cylindrical cup or trumpet in the center. The flowers may be yellow, gold, orange, white, or more rarely pinkish or green shades—or a combination of colors. In some, the petals and/or the trumpet and sometimes the reproductive parts have become doubled.

Height 6 to 14 in. (15 to 35 cm)
Hardiness Z4 or 5

DAFFODILS are among the most popular and easiest to grow of spring bulbs—if you avoid the more esoteric species types. As with other spring bulbs, planting in clumps in improved soil will ensure speedy establishment and the development of the clump as the bulbs multiply. A liquid feed or two after flowering will help build up the bulbs to flower well the following year.

The stout, strong stems of *Narcissus* 'Jack Snipe' hold up well in dry shade and provide sturdy support for the bicolored flowers.

'February Gold' is a classic early daffodil that flowers before deciduous trees have begun to leaf out. It soon multiplies into good-sized clumps.

In dry shade, the flowering stems may be less robust than normal; the shorter they are, the less likely they are to be broken in the wind and the more likely they are to support the flowers effectively. Plant hostas alongside the daffodil clumps so the maturing hosta foliage hides dying daffodil leaves.

To ensure the stems are not overloaded, choose smaller types with single flowers. Avoid those with double flowers and those with especially large flowers—these will usually be the big, yellow trumpet-flowered types. Avoid, too, those with a large number of flowers in a head unless they have good stout stems. Those listed here are a brief choice of the best robust, shorter, smaller flowered cultivars. If you prefer, ignore my choices and plant your personal favorites—but, please, no pre-packaged mixtures.

RECOMMENDED SELECTIONS

Narcissus **'Baby Moon'** Up to six deep yellow, fragrant flowers with the oval petals elegantly separated. 6 in. (15 cm) Z5

Narcissus **'February Gold'** Two-tone yellow, with slightly backswept petals and a fringed cup. 1 ft. (30 cm) Z4

Narcissus **'Ice Wings'** Up to four fragrant white flowers on strong stems. 1 ft. (30 cm) Z4

Narcissus **'Jack Snipe'** Has slightly backswept white petals and a yellow cup. 10 in. (25 cm) Z4

Narcissus **'Jenny'** Backswept white petals and a creamy cup; colonizes well. 1 ft. (30 cm) Z4

Narcissus **'Silver Chimes'** Noticeably olive-green leaves, clusters of nodding flowers with white petals and lemony cups. 1 ft. (30 cm) Z5

Narcissus **'Sun Disc'** Distinctive, evenly rounded disc of yellow petals with a flattened yellow cup. 6 in. (15 cm) Z4

Narcissus **'Thalia'** Has starry white petals and a white trumpet. 14 in. (38 cm) Z4

Corydalis sempervirens ROCK HARLEQUIN

Delightful slender annual for foliage and flower

A winter annual, with slightly succulent roots that support a loose rosette of blue-green, repeatedly divided leaves shaped rather like those of flat-leaved parsley. This overwinters and in spring sends up more or less vertical shoots, branching towards the top, carrying similar blue-green divided leaves and, from the leaf joints, sprays of yellow-tipped pink flowers about ½ in. (12 mm) long each with a single spur. These are followed by slender seed capsules up to 2 in (5 cm) long.

Height 12 to 15 in. (30 to 38 cm)
Hardiness Z3

PREVIOUS Foxglove, *Digitalis purpurea*, and rock harlequin, *Corydalis sempervirens*, are two short-lived plants that overwinter to provide a colorful spring display.

THIS DAINTY and attractive little annual of northern American forests tends to be most often seen in the wild on disturbed soil, especially after a fire. Fortunately, in the garden it is less particular in its habits. Its prettily divided blue-green rosettes add a distinctive coloring to the winter garden, then its dainty little bicolored flowers sway through late spring. Just this one attractive annual species is usually found, the flower color may vary slightly but the rare white flowered form is exactly that—rare. Flower color deepens with age.

In areas with cold winters and short springs, this under-rated plant tends to behave as a winter annual; in areas with a more prolonged spring, such as Britain and the Pacific Northwest, it may germinate in spring and flower in summer.

Rock harlequin is now endangered in some parts of its natural range, perhaps partly because forest fires are more ruthlessly controlled. Seed may not be easy to find but a web search will reveal sources, usually with smaller seed suppliers. You can sometimes find plants for sale, too. *Corydalis aurea* (scrambled eggs) is shorter, with yellow flowers, but seed is also difficult to find.

Planted far too rarely, the American native *Corydalis sempervirens* not only features these delightful bicolored flowers but its slightly bluish rosettes are an attractive winter or spring feature.

Digitalis purpurea

Perhaps the most colorful of dry shade plants

Foxgloves are biennials or short-lived perennials that produce a bold rosette of rough, slightly hairy, oval or more narrow, usually dark green leaves up to 10 in. (25 cm) long. In early summer, tall spikes of up to 80 flowers appear, each flower a tube up to 3 in. (7.5 cm) long. In wild types, the flowers line one side of the stem and tend to hang down; in some garden forms they are carried all round the stem and face outwards. Colors now available include white, pink, purple, cream, and yellow—sometimes with speckles or blotches in the throat. Most self-seed generously.

Height 3 to 5ft. (1 to 1.5 m)
Hardiness Z4

CLASSIC WILD and heirloom foxgloves do particularly well in dry shade. Their broad wintergreen rosettes soak up light and moisture when it is available and eventually turn it into impressive colorful spikes. Many gardeners prefer the shorter, very natural wild forms, which have one-sided, spotted white or purple spikes that turn over slightly at the tips. Indeed, the spotted white is one of the most lovely of all border plants.

Modern selections and hybrids can also work well for gardeners who prefer the punchier, more highly developed form, which have larger flowers packed all around long spikes. But these may become top-heavy in dry shade. Excelsior Group, with tall, imposing spikes in many colors seems tempting, but the plants are too tall to support themselves effectively in dry, low-light conditions. Some intriguing forms with very bold blotches in the throat or unusual flowers split into segments are also now available. You should be aware that all parts of foxgloves are toxic if eaten—but then why would you eat them?

To get plants off to a good start, sow seed in late spring in rich soil in a sunny spot in the garden, then transplant the seedlings to their final home in fall. Once growth is established, you can be sure of self-sown seedlings turning up and, in the fall, you can move them to where they are most needed. But be aware that if you have more than one form in the garden (or if there are other forms in nearby gardens) the bees will ensure that the next generation includes seedlings unlike their parents.

RECOMMENDED SELECTIONS

Digitalis purpurea **f. *albiflora*** White forms, some spotted, but with wild-style, one-sided spikes. 3 to 4 ft. (1 to 1.2 m)
Digitalis purpurea **Camelot Series** Prolific modern F1

My favorite form of all the foxgloves is this white variety, *Digitalis purpurea* f. *albiflora*.
The throat of each individual flower is prettily speckled with crimson spots.

hybrid series in four colors with large flowers all around the spike. 3 to 4 ft. (1 to 1.2 m)

Digitalis purpurea **Foxy Group** Shorter, all-round-the-spike flowers in many colors; usually sold as an unpredictable mixture. 3 ft. (1 m)

Digitalis purpurea **'Snow Thimble'** Wild type with pure white, unspotted flowers. 3 to 4 ft. (1 to 1.2 m)

Digitalis purpurea **'Sutton's Apricot'** One-sided spikes in apricot pink with ghostly spotting. 3 to 4 ft. (1 to 1.2 m)

Lunaria annua HONESTY

Robust biennial with colorful flowers and long-lasting seed heads

Honesty has a bold rosette of rough, heart-shaped, coarsely toothed, relatively pale green leaves that overwinters. In spring, upright stems emerge from this rosette topped with broad, colorful, leafy sprays of four-petaled, purple flowers. In poor soils, the stems are relatively unbranched, although a long-stalked cluster develops at each upper leaf joint so the result can be impressive. In richer conditions, leafy side shoots may break out low on the plant to create a broad, bushy, and colorful plant. Later, the seed heads develop; these flat, round, brown pods about 2 in. (5 cm) across reveal their silvery inner membrane when the outer skins fall away.

Height 2 to 3 ft. (60 to 90 cm)
Hardiness Z5

ONCE YOU HAVE one of the forms of this classic cottage garden flower, and they are all good, it is unlikely you will ever be without it. Honesty dependably blooms in the garden, it is colorful (though not long-lasting) when cut fresh for arrangements and, with its papery seedheads, is one of the best and easiest plants to grow for drying. And it will

Lunaria annua, in its range of shades from dark purple to pale purple to white, is an invaluable dry shade biennial whose deep green foliage rosettes also pack a punch.

ANNUALS AND BIENNIALS **185**

The seed pods of honesty, *Lunaria annua*, lose their purplish tones as they mature and develop into a long lasting silvery membrane that can be displayed in cut flower arrangements.

not object to dry shade although it may self-sow less prolifically in these conditions. Perhaps that is not a bad thing; those leafy rosettes can smother less forceful neighbors.

Only five forms are usually grown, all produce the same papery seedheads. There are three flower colors, and the foliage of two of them also comes in variegated forms. They all come true from seed if grown in isolation from each other; if you grow them all together the variegation tends to disappear as plants intercross and self-sown seedlings themselves self-sow as they mature. There is also very rare form called 'Corfu Blue', said to have blue flowers, but I have not yet seen it so cannot confirm the surprising coloring.

Thanks to the round, flat seedheads, *Lunaria annua* is sometimes called the money plant, silver dollar, and altogether more charmingly, moonwort. It may be a familiar and widely grown plant whose very ubiquity provokes disdain or, at best, disinterest. But honesty remains worth growing.

RECOMMENDED SELECTION

Lunaria annua The widely grown "unimproved" species has purple flowers; var. *albiflora* has pure white flowers; 'Alba Variegata' has white flowers and white-edged leaves; 'Munstead Purple' has the darkest reddish purple flowers; 'Variegata' has purple flowers and white-edged leaves.

NATIVE PLANTS

**British native plants
suitable for dry shade**

Arum italicum
Arum maculatum
Carex pendula
Digitalis purpurea
Dryopteris affinis
Dryopteris filix-mas
Fragaria vesca
Galium odoratum
Hedera helix
Helleborus foetidus
Ilex aquifolium
Iris foetidissima
Lamium galeobdolon
Luzula sylvatica
Polystichum aculeatum
Polystichum setiferum
Ruscus aculeatus

**North American
native plants suitable
for dry shade**

Carex appalachica
Carex pensylvanica
Corydalis sempervirens
Dryopteris filix-mas
Dryopteris marginalis
Fragaria chiloensis
Fragaria virginiana
Gaultheria shallon
Heuchera villosa
Ilex opaca
Mahonia aquifolium
Pachysandra procumbens
Parthenocissus quinquefolia
Polystichum acrostichoides
Polystichum munitum

SUGGESTIONS FOR FURTHER READING

This is the first book about plants for dry shade, so there are relatively few other publications to recommend. However, these books of mine will prove helpful.

Rice, Graham. *American Horticultural Society Encyclopedia of Perennials: The Definitive Illustrated Reference Guide*. New York: Dorling Kindersley, 2006.

Rice, Graham. *The Planting Planner*. London: Macmillan, 1996.

Rice, Graham. *Plants for Problem Places*. Portland, Oregon: Timber Press, 1988.

Rice, Graham. *Royal Horticultural Society Encyclopedia of Perennials: The Definitive Illustrated Reference Guide*. London: Dorling Kindersley, 2006.

These books are also well worth consulting:

Brown, George E. *Shade Plants for Garden and Woodland*. London: Faber, 1980.

Brown, George E. and Tony Kirkham. *The Pruning of Trees, Shrubs and Conifers*. Portland, Oregon: Timber Press, 2004.

Darke, Rick. *The American Woodland Garden*. Portland, Oregon: Timber Press, 2002.

Druse, Ken. *The Natural Shade Garden*. New York: Clarkson Potter, 1992.

Horn, Henry S. *The Adaptive Geometry of Trees*. Princeton, New Jersey, Princeton University Press, 1971.

Peattie, Donald Culross. *A Natural History of the Trees of Eastern and Central North America*. Boston, Massachusetts, 1977.

Wiley, Keith. Shade: *Planting Solutions for Shady Gardens*. Portland, Oregon: Timber Press, 2006.

INDEX

Graham Rice trained in horticulture at the prestigious Royal Botanic Gardens, Kew, England. A noted journalist, Graham has covered gardening for many major newspapers and magazines including *The Observer* and the *Evening Standard* in the UK, and written for *Horticulture* and *Garden Design* in the U.S. He is the author of more than 20 books, including *The Sweet Pea Book* (Timber Press) and his *Encyclopedia of Perennials*, published in separate Royal Horticultural Society and American Horticultural Society editions. He has the rare distinction of winning garden writing awards on both sides of the Atlantic, including from the Garden Writers Association of America and the Garden Media Guild of the UK. Graham has recently been honored with the International Contributor Award from the Perennial Plant Association. He is a prolific blogger; his blog, TransatlanticGardener.com was runner up for Garden Blog of The Year, and his New Plants blog for the Royal Horticultural Society is keenly followed. He recently launched a series of eBooks.

Graham judges at the world famous Chelsea Flower Show, is a member of a number of Royal Horticultural Society committees, and judges the RHS flower trials throughout the year.

He divides his gardening time between Pennsylvania and England with his wife, American garden writer/photographer judywhite. Most of their garden is shaded, and they have grown (and killed) a wide variety of plants searching for those which will also withstand the dry conditions. When not in the garden or at his desk, Graham hosts a music show, The BritMix, for a public radio station. Photo by judywhite/GardenPhotos.com